JESUIT SATURDAYS

SHARING THE IGNATIAN SPIRIT

with Friends and Colleagues

Faith is the eye of love.

Also by William J. Byron, SJ

Toward Stewardship (1975)

The Causes of World Hunger (editor, 1982)

Quadrangle Considerations (1989)

Take Your Diploma and Run! (1992)

Take Courage: Psalms of Support and Encouragement (editor, 1995)

Finding Work without Losing Heart (1995)

The 365 Days of Christmas (1996)

Answers from Within (1998)

A Book of Quiet Prayer (2006)

Individuarian Observations (2007)

Praying with and for Others (2008)

JESUIT SATURDAYS

SHARING THE IGNATIAN SPIRIT

with Friends and Colleagues

William J. Byron, SJ

Foreword by Vincent T. O'Keefe, SJ
Foreword to the New and Revised Edition by James Martin, SJ

LOYOLA PRESS.
A JESUIT MINISTRY
Chicago

LOYOLA PRESS.
A JESUIT MINISTRY

3441 N. Ashland Avenue
Chicago, Illinois 60657
(800) 621-1008
www.loyolapress.com

Cover design by Think Design Group LLC
Interior design by Maggie Hong

Paperback ISBN 978-0-8294-2718-9
Hardcover ISBN 978-0-8294-1468-4

Library of Congress Cataloging-in-Publication Data
Byron, William J., 1927–
   Jesuit Saturdays : sharing the Ignatian spirit with friends and lay colleagues / William J. Byron ; foreword by Vincent T. O'Keefe.
    p. cm.
   Includes bibliographical references.
   ISBN 0-8294-1468-1 (hardcover)
   1. Jesuits.   2. Byron, William J., 1927–   I. Title.
BX3702.2 .B97 2000
255'.53—dc21
                              99-055854

Printed in the United States of America
08 09 10 11 12 13 Versa 10 9 8 7 6 5 4 3 2 1

TO THE MEMORY OF

John V. McEvoy, SJ,
who, as master of novices,
introduced me to the Jesuit way of life

CONTENTS

Foreword   ix

Foreword to the New and Revised Edition   xi

Acknowledgments   xiii

Introduction   xv

CHAPTER 1   The Man Who Was Loyola   1

CHAPTER 2   Why We Are in Higher Education   11

CHAPTER 3   Why We Are in Secondary Education   23

CHAPTER 4   Education for Social Justice   35

CHAPTER 5   The Enduring Evidence of a Jesuit Education   47

CHAPTER 6   Discernment: A Spirituality of Choice   59

CHAPTER 7   Living Generously in the Service of Others   77

CHAPTER 8   The Celibate: A Crowd of One   91

CHAPTER 9   Individuarians   103

CHAPTER 10   Stewardship: The Jesuit Approach to the Use of Wealth, Power, and Talent   117

CHAPTER 11   The Standard of Christ   129

CHAPTER 12   The Harvest Is Ready   141

Epilogue   157

Endnotes   161

About the Author   169

FOREWORD

General Congregations for Jesuits are both important—they are the highest legislative body—and infrequent; since 1540 there have been only thirty-four of them. There is an obvious need for one when the superior general dies and a new one has to be elected. Such was the case for twenty-six of these congregations. On only eight occasions was the congregation summoned for "matters of greater moment." This was true of the Thirty-Fourth General Congregation (GC 34) in 1995, which reflected carefully and prayerfully on the life of the Society from 1965 to 1995, a truly momentous period in the life of the Church and of society in general. The main thrust, however, was to the future and to setting out those orientations needed by all Jesuits as they enter a new century.

A key document of GC 34 entitled "Cooperation with the Laity in Mission" went to the heart of the Society's apostolic action: "Cooperation with the laity is both a constitutive element of our way of proceeding and a grace calling for individual, communal, and institutional renewal. It invites us to service of the ministry of lay people, partnership with them in mission, and openness to creative ways of future cooperation" (decree 13, no. 26).

Such a document, written for a worldwide group, had to be broad enough to cover widely divergent situations. This created a pressing need for someone to spell out the implications of this document for the local scene. What does "partnership with the laity in mission" mean in the United States? It is precisely to this felt need that Father Bill Byron responds in his engaging and delightful book, which will be of great use to lay colleagues who are associated with Jesuits in so many different endeavors.

I am thinking particularly of our Jesuit educational institutions so caught up in discussions of Jesuit mission and identity, and how this book will be of great help to trustees, faculty, administrators, and staff, as well as to students and alumni. We Jesuits have been negligent in communicating to the many laypeople associated with us in a host of activities in schools, parishes, retreat houses, social centers, publishing houses, research centers, etc., who we are, what we do, and what people can expect of us. We need to explain what we mean by our expression *our way of proceeding* if we expect others to enter into a partnership with us.

In a style that is personal and enlightening as well as inviting to discussion and conversation, Father Byron shares with us a vision of Jesuit life today as seen and lived by a man of uncommonly rich experience. This book will appeal to a large and varied audience, but the two chapters on higher and secondary education will have a special appeal for those involved in educational institutions. This is the type of book that administrators, especially those concerned with the vital topic of Jesuit mission and identity, will want to make available to many people in their institutions. It will provide a natural basis for discussion and conversation. Jesuits will enjoy it and will want to share it with their colleagues as they work toward a partnership in mission. I would find it an excellent reference for young men interested in learning more about Jesuit life.

The publication of this volume will be a fitting way for Father Bill Byron to celebrate his golden jubilee as a member of the Society of Jesus during the great Jubilee Year of the Church.

Vincent T. O'Keefe, SJ
Superior of the Jesuit Community
at America House in New York City
General Assistant to
Superior General Pedro Arrupe, SJ, 1965–83

FOREWORD TO THE
NEW AND REVISED EDITION

Far be it from me to add anything to what Vincent T. O'Keefe, SJ, wrote in his original foreword! Fathers O'Keefe and Byron are among the most esteemed of all American Jesuits: they have, between them, decades of experience in Catholic education (both served as presidents of Catholic universities) as well as in a host of Jesuit ministries.

But perhaps I can underline one aspect that Father O'Keefe mentioned in his foreword. He noted that Jesuits have been generally negligent in communicating to our lay colleagues "our way of proceeding." St. Ignatius of Loyola used that phrase time and again in his writings, both personal and official. It's an expression that has come to mean not only the way that Jesuits carry out our work and make decisions, but also the way that we look at the world. And there are few people who can communicate our way of proceeding better than William J. Byron, SJ.

Among the Jesuits, Bill is widely known not only as an optimistic man, an affable priest, and a prayerful Christian—but also as an extraordinarily dedicated worker. He is indefatigable! Just glance at the back of this book under the section entitled "About the Author" to see what I mean. Father Byron is a true laborer in the vineyard of the Lord.

But, as this marvelous book demonstrates, a good Jesuit is not simply someone who works hard. He is also someone who finds God in all things. That is, he is someone who prays. According to

Jesuit tradition, he is a "contemplative in action." This is the heart of our way of proceeding.

With his justly popular book *Jesuit Saturdays*, Father Byron offers an invitation to live out this ideal—the contemplative in action—to the men and women who work with the Jesuits in a variety of settings. And with this new paperback edition an even greater number of people will be encouraged to participate in the vision of St. Ignatius, which was designed not simply for Jesuit priests and brothers but for all men and women. Indeed, laypersons were among the very first people to whom St. Ignatius offered his famous Spiritual Exercises, his four-week plan for prayer, in the sixteenth century.

Members of the Society of Jesus sometimes use the expression "ours" to connote a Jesuit or a Jesuit ministry. We will say, "That's one of *our* schools." Or we will say, "That guy is one of *ours*." Sometimes the phrase is even capitalized to emphasize its importance! Lately this expression has been criticized as being somewhat proprietary, somewhat insular, and somewhat exclusive. But, over the past few years, I've grown more and more fond of that word, especially when it comes to those apostolates, ministries, and institutions founded by Jesuits.

Here's why: For the past few decades Jesuits have worked side by side with our lay colleagues. More to the point, they often work *for* them! So these ministries—colleges, universities, middle schools, high schools, parishes, retreat centers, and many more—really are *ours*.

In a very real way, they are *all of ours*.

So is the vision that Father Byron introduces in this book. May you find in these pages further inspiration for our work, a greater understanding of our way of proceeding, a deeper knowledge of our Ignatian spirituality, and, overall, a more profound relationship with our God.

James Martin, SJ
July 31, 2008
Feast of Saint Ignatius of Loyola

ACKNOWLEDGMENTS

My thanks for permissions received from the Woodstock Center
for Theological Reflection to reprint the summary explanation by
James L. Connor, SJ, of the Spiritual Exercises and the Examen;
the Institute of Jesuit Sources to use the cited material from
Candido de Dalmases, SJ, *Ignatius of Loyola: Founder of the Jesuits*
(1985); Loyola College in Maryland to quote from the report of
that institution's Middle States Working Group on Jesuit and
Catholic Identity; Joseph A. Califano Jr. to quote excerpts from his
speech on Jesuit secondary education (reprinted in *America*, May
25, 1996, and used here with the permission of America Press);
James P. M. Walsh, SJ, to reprint his February 7, 1993, letter to
the *Washington Post*; the Center for Ignatian Spirituality at Boston
College to quote from its brochure *What Is Ignatian Spirituality?*;
Schocken Books to quote from Harold Kushner, *When Bad Things
Happen to Good People* (1981); George W. Traub, SJ, to quote
from his glossary of terms used in Ignatian and Jesuit circles, *Do
You Speak Ignatian?*; and James J. Gill, SJ, to use portions of his
December 1969 interview in *Medical Insight*.

I am particularly grateful to Vincent T. O'Keefe, SJ, and James
Martin, SJ, for their generous forewords and for help with this
project received from other Jesuit friends, notably Jim Connor, Jim
Walsh, and Jerry Cavanagh. Maureen Waldron and Dean Hoge
read the manuscript, and their comments helped to improve the
final product.

George Lane, SJ, Linda Schlafer, and Belinda Duvel of Loyola
Press provided welcome support and editorial encouragement;

they set an excellent example for Jesuit-lay cooperation. Countless others have helped along the way. All I can say is, "Thanks," and in doing so, I acknowledge that I am thereby declaring myself to be "much obliged." And, with this new and revised paperback edition, I extend my thanks to Joe Durepos, executive editor, trade acquisitions, of Loyola Press, for making this possible.

INTRODUCTION

Fifty years a Jesuit. July 31, 2000, is the marker for me. Fifty years a Jesuit and, as I've found myself remarking in recent years, I've never had a really unhappy day in the Jesuit order, the Company that was founded by the grace of God and the genius of Ignatius of Loyola in 1540. I've had difficult, even painful, days in the Society of Jesus, but I've never had a fundamentally unhappy one.

Now, with the publication of this paperback edition, it is almost sixty years a Jesuit for me. I wouldn't change anything in that opening paragraph, taken from the first edition, except to identify the pain I, along with all Jesuits and so many colleagues and friends, experienced when news of the clergy sex abuse scandal broke in America in 2002. I would also add the discouraging fact that additional Jesuits have left "the Company" since the year 2000 and fewer have joined. So I was both impressed and encouraged to note that when Spanish-born Father Adolfo Nicolas, SJ, was elected superior general of the Society of Jesus in January 2008, the Catholic News Service in the U.S. lifted the following words from an interview appearing in the newsletter of the Australian Jesuits that Father Nicolas had given the month before. Father Nicolas asked:

> The question for us is: Is it enough that we are happy with our life and are improving our service and ministry? Isn't there also an important factor in the perception of people ('vox populi') that should drive us to some deeper

reflection on religious life today? How come we elicit so
much admiration and so little following?

This is a book of personal reflections similar to those I published
as *Quadrangle Considerations* and the commencement-address
chapters in *Take Your Diploma and Run: Speaking to the Next
Generation*.[1] The present book is not an autobiography, although
personal experience is part of the story. It is simply one Jesuit's
perspective on aspects of Jesuit life that appear to be of growing
interest to others, particularly lay colleagues and friends. The primary audience I have in mind is the group of committed laypeople
I've met worldwide who serve as trustees, faculty, staff, and support personnel in Jesuit educational institutions, parishes, research
and retreat centers, publishing operations, and other ministries. I
speak to students, alumni, parishioners, retreatants, benefactors,
and friends—all those people who cast their lot in one way or
another with Jesuits. I hope that this book will also be helpful to
young men who are in the process of discerning whether God is
calling them to Jesuit life.

So many people in various partnering or associative relationships with Jesuits want to know what it is that makes us tick; they
are curious about who we are and what we do. They are quite
open these days in asking us to tell them more about ourselves. My
students often heard me say, "You are the world's leading expert
on your own opinion" when I invited expressions of opinion in the
classroom or in written assignments. The only area of expertise I
can claim is related to my own opinions and experiences, so I offer
them here simply for what they are worth, to lay friends who want
to better understand the Jesuit way, style, approach, and tradition.

Why the title *Jesuit Saturdays*? Because Saturdays (every one, in
the Jesuit tradition, a day of special devotion to Mary, the mother
of Jesus) have always been an important part of my Jesuit life. On
Saturday afternoons during my novitiate ("boot camp" or "basic
training") from 1950 to 1952 at the Novitiate of St. Isaac Jogues,

Wernersville, Pennsylvania, other novices and I would go off on missions to the Berks County Jail or to what was then known as the "Negro section" of the nearby city of Reading (the fictional Brewer in John Updike's Rabbit novels) to teach catechism and engage in some form of social ministry. Seeds planted within me then grew into subsequent academic degrees in economics, a life-long interest in social ethics, and an abiding concern for interracial and social justice.

At every stage of my Jesuit life, Saturdays have allowed some extra time and freedom for writing and reflection that the week-day press of study, teaching, or administrivia did not permit. From 1953 to 1956, as a Jesuit scholastic studying philosophy at Saint Louis University, I walked through a lot of poor neighborhoods on Saturday afternoons and often made hospital visits with, I must confess, the mixed motivation of seeing sick patients and watching with them the televised sporting events not available for viewing on Saturday afternoons in the somber scholasticate of that era.

Once ordained in 1961, after three years of theological studies at Woodstock College in Maryland, my classmates and I stayed on as "fourth-year fathers" for a final year of weekday study and week-end ministry in hospitals and parishes in the nearby Baltimore-Washington area. That initiation into ordained pastoral ministry, especially hearing confessions on Saturdays and preaching to large congregations of practicing Catholics on Sundays, was, for all of us, the realization of a deep and genuine vocational desire. And being able to catch an occasional Baltimore Colts or Orioles game before making the photo-finish return trip to rural Woodstock in time for Sunday vespers was, for us young priests, all part of the hundredfold.

Saturdays became regular writing days for me in 1973 when, well after graduate study for a degree in economics and several years of teaching economics (at Loyola in Maryland) and social ethics (at Woodstock), I became dean of arts and sciences at Loyola University in New Orleans. I got into the habit of doing what I enjoy, namely, sitting down at the keyboard after break-fast on Saturday mornings (ranging over the years from manual to electric typewriter, to word processor, to personal computer) and writing until an early afternoon lunch break followed by a long walk (occasionally interrupted by a good movie). These Jesuit Saturdays produced a few books and a lot of essays over the years. The memory of those days is special to me, and the eventually published products of that reflection have been helpful to others.

The idea for writing this book came to me during an extraordinary three-day meeting of business education professionals on the campus of Seattle University in July 1998. They gathered at the invitation of Jesuit Father Robert Spitzer, then professor of philosophy at Seattle University and now president of Gonzaga University in Spokane, and his Seattle faculty colleague Dr. Karen Brown, chair of the department of management. Well aware that modern Jesuits are committed to educating men and women for others, this impressive array of fifty or so deans and faculty members from Jesuit business schools across the country came together to share their views on planning curriculum, teaching business ethics, organizing service learning, and integrating spirituality into business practice. They gathered to reflect together not only on the relevance of all this to the Jesuit spirit of the institutions they serve but also on the expected impact of the Jesuit character of those institutions on their teaching and research.

It seems to have worked. The first edition of *Jesuit Saturdays* found its way into orientation packets for new faculty at Jesuit prep schools and colleges, into the boardrooms of Jesuit institutions, onto the bookshelves of retreat house and parish libraries, and into the hands of young men trying to discern whether God might be calling them to join the order.

It was my hope in writing this book—and that same hope remains strong as this revised edition goes to press—that these pages will present an honest portrait of Jesuit life along with an introduction to Ignatian spirituality.

I also want to convey here my admiration and gratitude to those generous and dedicated lay colleagues who energize our Jesuit works today. In them the Ignatian spirit is evident; without them the Jesuit institutions, so well known and loved by so many for so long, could not survive.

CHAPTER 1

The Man Who Was Loyola

I've seen the Loyola name all over the world—on businesses like banks and restaurants, on streets, and, most frequently, on schools at every level of education. The name *St. Ignatius* is similarly attached to schools and parish churches everywhere.

From the proper noun *Ignatius* comes the adjective *Ignatian*, which identifies a spirituality and spirit that reflect the soul of the founder of the Jesuits. Many lay colleagues who work with Jesuits, especially those not of the Catholic faith, are naturally curious about the man behind the name of the institutions where they work. Something is usually said to address that curiosity during orientation sessions for newcomers to faculty and staff positions at Jesuit institutions.

Students, too, occasionally wonder about the person behind the name on their diplomas (if they went to one of the many Loyolas) or behind the "spirit" often mentioned as a special characteristic of Jesuit schools. In an address to the midyear graduating class at Loyola University of Chicago, I decided to speak about the man who was Loyola—St. Ignatius of Loyola—after whom every Loyola college or university is named. Even if the school bears another name, Loyola will always be connected to the lives and careers of every Jesuit-school graduate once the degree is conferred. So, I thought, why not take a few moments at a Loyola commencement to say something about the man who was Loyola? And why not do that now in these pages to introduce lay associates to the person who started the whole Jesuit enterprise?

Iñigo Lopez de Loyola was born in 1491; Loyola was the name of his ancestors' manor house and farmland in northern Spain, the Basque country. The surnames of the Basques derived from the house or estate to which they belonged. *Iñigo* was his given name; he later changed it to *Ignatius*, probably out of admiration for the great Christian martyr Ignatius of Antioch. *Ignatius* is not, as many suppose, a translation of the name *Iñigo* to another language.

His family was large and wealthy. Iñigo and his brothers were, in various capacities, in service to the kings of Castile. The young Iñigo might best be described as a courtier; some writers refer to him as a knight. His earliest biographer, Ribandeneira, describes him as "a lively and trim young man, very fond of court dress and good living."[1]

Breaking with the Past

Iñigo, although never a full-time professional soldier, is often referred to as the Soldier Saint. He was seriously wounded by the French at Pamplona in May of 1521 when a cannonball shattered his right leg and wounded his left. Immediate medical attention was crude, hasty, and obviously ineffective; he was sent home on a litter to the castle of his ancestors. The bones, Iñigo writes in his third-person *Autobiography*, "either because they had been badly set or because the jogging of the journey had displaced them, would not heal. Again he went through this butchery [a reference to the repeat surgery] in which, as in all the others that he suffered before or after, he uttered not a word nor showed any sign of pain other than the tight clenching of fists."[2] During a long recuperation, the future saint had what he describes as his first reasoning, his first reflective experience, on the things of God. You will read more about this experience in chapter 6.

Upon recovery from his wounds and related illness, Iñigo resolved to follow Christ. He made his way to the Benedictine monastery at Montserrat in Spain, sought out a confessor, and unburdened his soul in a three-day general confession. Then he hung up his sword and dagger—emblems of a swashbuckling past—at the famous Montserrat Marian Shrine of the Black Virgin (stained black from years of candle smoke rising from below). His intention, according to a recent historical account, was "to clothe himself there with the arms of his new spiritual warfare, in the fashion of young knights who entered upon the service of earthly warfare."[3]

He left Montserrat intending to go directly to Barcelona to board a ship for the Holy Land to visit—as he had resolved to do during his recuperation—the places made holy by the footprints and eventually the blood of Jesus. But he delayed for eleven months in the village of Manresa (another famous place-name in Jesuit history), about twenty miles from Montserrat, where he experienced interior trials as well as divine illuminations. At Manresa, he underwent a spiritual transformation, an experience he would later draw upon in producing his *Spiritual Exercises*, a handbook intended to serve as an outline for a monthlong retreat. He would later invite Francis Xavier and other individuals of "magnanimity and generosity" to make the Exercises, which were designed to help them, by God's grace, become even more generous. In the introduction to this handbook, Ignatius writes, "We call Spiritual Exercises every way of preparing and disposing the soul to rid itself of all inordinate attachments, and, after their removal, of seeking and finding the will of God in the disposition of our life for the salvation of our soul" (*SpEx*, 1).[4] The salvation of others—what Ignatius constantly refers to in later apostolic planning as the "help of souls," or service—was never far from his thoughts. But the beginning experience of the Exercises focuses on the cultivation, by God's action in the soul, of a fuller freedom and closer union with God on the part of the one who would be, in the Ignatian mode, a follower of Christ. Ignatius had a vision, a commitment, and a pattern of living that eventually became known worldwide as the Jesuit way of life. Every Jesuit school, college, and university has been touched by that influence.

Several short paragraphs at the beginning of the book constitute what Ignatius calls the "First Principle and Foundation" of
the Spiritual Exercises. These words have been pondered often
and deeply by every Jesuit throughout his Jesuit life. They help to
explain why Jesuits do what they do, including establishing the
institutions that bear the name *Loyola*. These words can serve
as a personal mission statement for those who see life and faith
from a Jesuit perspective. Here is what Ignatius would say to
a young graduate or anyone associating him- or herself with a
Jesuit work:

> You are created to praise, reverence, and serve God your
> Lord, and by this means to save your soul.
>
> The other things on the face of the earth are created
> for you to help you in attaining the end for which you are
> created.
>
> Hence, you are to make use of them in as far as they help
> you in the attainment of your end, and you must rid yourself
> of them in as far as they prove a hindrance to you.
>
> Therefore, you must make yourself indifferent to all
> created things, as far as you are allowed free choice and are
> not under any prohibition. Consequently, as far as you are
> concerned, you should not prefer health to sickness, riches
> to poverty, honor to dishonor, a long life to a short life. The
> same holds for all other things.
>
> Your one desire and choice should be what is more condu-
> cive to the end for which you are created. (*SpEx*, 23)

It takes spiritual maturity to catch the Ignatian vision, to see the
"First Principle and Foundation" as a basis for living, as a focus
that helps you find God and God's love in all things. It takes additional spiritual maturity to be willing to make your own the famous
Ignatian prayer for generosity: "Dear Lord, teach me to be generous; teach me to serve you as you deserve to be served; to give and
not to count the cost; to fight and not to heed the wounds; to toil

and not to seek for rest; to labor and not to ask for any reward, save that of knowing that I am doing your will, O God."[5]

Contemplatives in Action

The man who was Loyola had a tendency to see life as a struggle between the forces of good and the forces of evil. He was a mystic who saw the world from God's point of view. He founded his religious order—the Jesuits—for like-minded men called, as he was, to be contemplatives in action. Ignatius and his first companions committed themselves "to travel anywhere in the world where there is hope of God's greater glory and the good of souls." The phrase *God's greater glory* appears on the logo, the coat of arms, of many Jesuit institutions and organizations: *ad majorem Dei gloriam*. Ignatius understood that the greater glory of God involves a greater, more generous, and selfless service to others. For Ignatius, the help of souls meant the help of bodies too. Just as Mother Teresa of Calcutta did in the late twentieth century, he always sent his men to minister in hospitals, care for the poor, protect prostitutes and marginated people, and instruct unsophisticated children in religion.

Graduates leaving Jesuit campuses today are encouraged not to leave that spirit behind. In fact, they are often urged to take it upon themselves to learn more about the man and his vision. There are good biographies to be read. There are the Spiritual Exercises to be made (experienced, not read) at a Jesuit retreat house. And there is a daily opportunity to pray to the man who was Loyola for a share of his vision, generosity, and high-hearted love of God. If that prayer is answered, the person who makes it, young or old, will be off to a great start, a genuine commencement of the unique service to a human community in need of the help that only faith-committed and generous persons can bring. Moreover, if a person catches the Ignatian vision, the spirit of the man who was Loyola, he or she may be moved to pray from time to time as Ignatius prayed at the commencement of his apostolic life:

Take, Lord, and receive all my liberty, my memory, my understanding, and my entire will, all that I have and possess. You have given it all to me. To you, Lord, I return it. All of it is yours; dispose of it wholly according to your will. Give me only your love and your grace, and that will be enough for me. Amen.

H. O. Evennett refers to the Spiritual Exercises as "the systematized, demysticized quintessence of the process of Ignatius's own conversion and purposeful change of life."[6] The process was reduced to handbook form so that it would be available, generation after generation, to facilitate the same change in others. As an appendix to this chapter, I want to reproduce here—with the permission of Father James L. Connor, SJ, the author—a brief description of the Spiritual Exercises together with an explanation of the Ignatian examen, a form of prayer considered essential for those who would follow the spirituality Ignatius introduced to the life of the Church. Father Connor, when director of the Woodstock Center for Theological Reflection at Georgetown University, prepared this summary for those who attended a special Woodstock forum, "St. Ignatius's Spiritual Exercises: Woodstock's Way of Promoting Justice," in Washington, D.C., on November 12, 1998.

The Spiritual Exercises of St. Ignatius: What They Are

The *Spiritual Exercises* are a retreat of thirty days (with various adaptations in length and style) to assist people to understand how to discover, in the context of their daily life and worldly affairs, God's desires and will for them, and to be given the freedom to do it. Ideally, these exercises become, with practice and over time, an habitual *modus operandi*.

1. The *Spiritual Exercises* open with a consideration of *God's loving design for our world* and our role in its achievement. We are then invited to an initial evaluation of our

stewardship: our successes and failures in collaborating with God to realize his desires for us and our world.

2. For the most part the *Exercises* are a series of meditations on *select Scripture passages* which the retreatant reads, ponders, and prays over, in order to be informed, impressed, moved, and affected by them. The aim is to come *(a)* to understand Christ's mission: what it is *for* and what it fights *against* ("to know him more clearly"), *(b)* to admire him ("to love him more dearly"), and *(c)* to feel drawn to join with him in his struggle and to follow him on his mission ("to follow him more nearly"). These scriptural meditations move from Christ's birth and childhood, through his public ministry, to his passion, death, and resurrection. This is not just a chronology; there is, we discover, an unfolding "logic."

3. Interspersed throughout this series of scriptural meditations are *special exercises* which Ignatius has developed in order to clarify, illustrate, and dramatize (through use of imagination and affections) this struggle between the contending forces of good and evil, God and Satan, Jesus and the "world" (in St. John's sense of that word). We come to experience that this struggle is going on both "out there" in the world and "in here" in our own hearts and minds. Some of these special exercises are: viewing our world through the eyes of the Trinity; considering Christ's call to us as that of a warrior seeking companionship in battle (the young Ignatius was a soldier!); understanding the forces of good and evil as two sets of "campaign strategies"; and discovering, experiencing, and appreciating Christ as a "laborer" working here and now in history with and for us.

4. Also interspersed throughout the scriptural meditations are special exercises for testing, refining, and building up our *freedom* to choose the good. For instance, putting ourselves

on our death bed and looking back on the options we "faced";
giving advice to our best friend; grading ourselves on the
level or degree of our honesty and generosity; etc. There is
instruction about and exercises for getting in touch with our
feelings—which both energize us and reveal our motivations
to us as either worthy or unworthy, freeing us or binding us.

5. Instruction and guidance in *discernment of "spirits"* (i.e., the *sources* of feelings that are trying to motivate us to action) and *decision making,* i.e., in choosing the good to which God calls us. This process includes getting the relevant data, understanding and affirming it accurately, weighing or discerning the relative merits and value of the various possible courses of action in response to the needs or opportunity revealed in this concrete situation, making the decision which "seems best in the Lord," and carrying it into action. There are instructions about "Making an Election or a Choice of a State of Life," "Rules for the Discernment of Spirits," and doing the "Examen of Consciousness."

The Ignatian Examen

Some Presuppositions in Doing the Examen

1. God's creating is a continuing sharing of Trinitarian life with all creation "that they may all be one, as you, Father, are in me and I in you, that they also may be in us" (John 17:21).

2. Thus present in creation and human history, God guides us toward the full attainment of this life with God and one another in unity and peace, justice and love.

3. We humans can discern the direction of God's active guidance in our own daily history, and can collaborate with God to promote its realization in action.

4. The sign of God's guidance is: what produces unity and peace among people and what instills feelings of peace, love, and integrity in us. By contrast, what produces dissension and hostility in society and selfishness and vengeance in us is a sign of the presence and activity of evil. (See Galatians 5:13–26.)

Steps in Making the Ignatian Examen

1. We begin by quieting ourselves. Become aware of God's goodness, the gifts of life and love. Be thankful. Recall that without faith, the eye of love, the human world seems too evil for God to be good, for a good God to exist.

2. Pray for the grace to see clearly, to understand accurately, and to respond generously to the guidance God is giving us in our daily history.

3. Review in memory the history of the day (week, month, etc.) in order to be shown concrete instances of the presence and guidance of God and, perhaps, of the activity and influence of evil. These can be detected by paying attention to strong feelings we experienced that may have accompanied or arisen from situations and encounters.

4. Evaluate these instances in which we have either collaborated with God or yielded to the influence of evil in some way. Express gratitude and regret.

5. Plan and decide how to collaborate more effectively with God and how, with God's assistance, to avoid or overcome the influence of evil in the future.

6. Conclude with an Our Father.

1. Quiet
2. Pray for Grace
3. Review God's presence
4. Evaluate my acceptance
5. Plan for improvement
6. "Our Father"

CHAPTER 2

Why We Are in Higher Education

Central to any Jesuit work is the development of human potential.
The positive side of human potential, when you stop to think
about it, stretches into eternity—toward union with the Creator.
The negative side points to the possibility of eternal alienation—to
permanent frustration of that potential. Ignatius was well aware of
evil in the world, of the presence of "an enemy of human nature"
intent on deflecting unsuspecting men and women from their path
toward God.

Formal education's interests are coextensive with the entire
range of positive possibilities for human development. Throughout
their well more than 450-year history, Jesuits have recognized
this and have, almost from the beginning, chosen formal education—beginning at what we would call the secondary level—as
an extraordinarily valuable instrument for their work in the development of human potential. Higher education touches that range
of positive possibilities in a privileged way. Skills and maturity
acquired in primary and secondary stages of educational growth
make possible the conscious pursuit of wisdom. Not information
only, nor technique, nor accumulated experience, but wisdom is
a real possibility at the stage of human development associated
with higher education. At this level it is the privilege of educators to group themselves into communities of inquiry that may in
fact become or beget wisdom communities. At the level of higher

education, it is the responsibility of educators to work for the formation of wise and reflective human beings.

The Complementary Norms from the Society's 34th General Congregation express the official Jesuit answer to the question, Why are we in higher education?

> Universities and institutions of higher learning play an increasingly important role in the formation of the whole human community, for in them our culture is shaped by debates about ethics, future directions for economics and politics, and the very meaning of human existence. Accordingly, we must see to it that the Society is present in such institutions, whether directed by itself or by others, insofar as we are able to do so. It is crucial for the Church, therefore, that dedicated Jesuits continue to engage in University work. (*CN*, 289) [1]

Higher education is a medium, not just a means; it has intrinsic value. Involving, as it does, the pursuit of wisdom, higher education is worth much in purely human terms and is thus worthy of dedicated human effort. But the worth of higher education, as both means and medium, transcends the human and touches the divine. That is why, it seems to me, a completely secular university is not really a university. If closed to a faith dimension, to an exploration of the transcendent and an examination of revelation, a university is hardly universal in its interests and thus holds questionable claim to that name.

Moving Hearts and Minds

The Jesuit purpose in higher education is to move the minds and hearts of developing humans. The direction of this movement, in the Jesuit view, is Godward (which is why Jesuits think that theology is an essential part of a college education). The norm is truth (which is the rationale for including philosophy). The outcome, it is to be hoped, is wisdom (hence the importance of the humanities in Jesuit education). And wisdom, in the Jesuit understanding, is a gift from God that enables the recipient to understand what is really important in events past or present (the humanities help a student get into all of that). Although no one can predict the future, the wise man or woman, having experience in sorting out the truly significant in past and present events, is well positioned to make wise choices en route to an unknown future.

The Jesuit way in higher education is one of method and motivation. In the Jesuit view, learning is directed by a motivator-organizer and assimilated by an active participant in the learning process. Viewed in this way, learning is a self-propelled activity. The Jesuit educator tries, therefore, to move the minds and hearts of those who want to learn. Content is important, but it is secondary to knowing how to learn and wanting to learn more. Father James P. M. Walsh, SJ, longtime member of the theology department at Georgetown University, offered these useful reflections about students and teaching:

> Students are in process, developing. They can be encouraged and brought along in that process, and this should be done with kindness. This direction should be methodical, step-by-step guidance; students should not be left to tutor themselves. In this process students should be taken where they are, not where they "should" be; all education is remedial. Resistance to learning, when it shows up, is a precious opportunity for a teaching and learning moment. Savor and explore those occasions—that's where work needs to be done and progress can be made. But never be manipulative or have a hidden agenda, except for the agenda of helping the student develop those budding faculties of memory, imagination, reason, and self-knowledge, to the full flowering of the human being, created in the image of God.

Part of that work is the invitation to detect and poke at idols, without however giving students the sense that they have everything figured out or that they are somehow already in possession of the truth—that would indeed merit the millstone. It is uncomfortable always being a beginner, but that is the presupposition of being a learner, and Jesuit educational philosophy, as I understand it, tends to savor that "nescience," that sense of being at a loss but also having whole new worlds to explore: dismaying but exciting. And exploration of a focused, serious sort: students have to be taught how to engage complexity, how to follow a sustained argument, how to be led—and then discern.

The student is at the center of everything the Jesuit college or university wants to do.

As the Jesuit is a faith-committed person, so Jesuit education is intended to be a faith-committed activity. In all things, the Jesuit understands that the immediate task is his but the ultimate power to achieve that task belongs to God. This applies in matters practical and theoretical, in undertakings spiritual and physical, in efforts by individuals and groups. If, as faith directs, everything depends on God, then wisdom would suggest that everything must be entrusted to God. Such wisdom lies at the beginning and end of Jesuit education. And wisdom, it must be remembered, is a gift from God. Two verses from the book of Proverbs explain this characteristically Jesuit attitude: "Entrust your works to the LORD, / and your plans will succeed" (16:3) and "In his mind a man plans his course, / but the LORD / directs his steps" (16:9).

Father Raymond Baumhart, SJ, when president of Loyola University of Chicago, often remarked, "Loyola is certainly church-related, but since I spend a lot more time in Springfield [the state capital] than I do with the cardinal, I'm beginning to believe that for all practical purposes we're a lot more government-related than church-related." In any case, every Jesuit university, regardless of its degree of tilt toward church or state, is or should be clearly *faith*-committed.

Efficient and Effective

In education, as in all else, the Jesuit is not content with simple efficiency—doing something right. Rather, he wants to be effective, which means doing the right thing. Accordingly, in all things the Jesuit way involves a search for God's will. This search, in the Jesuit vocabulary, goes by the name of discernment. (One Jesuit I knew, the late Tom Savage, a professor of English at Xavier University in Cincinnati, taught his students a lot about discernment by means of a simple message posted on his office door: "The fool collects, the wise person chooses.") Discernment, it should be noted, is a wisdom characteristic that prepares a person to choose wisely. Chapter 6 will develop that theme in more detail.

Jesuits in higher education will, upon reflection, notice that their method, their style, their way of doing what they do, is radically influenced by the spirit of their founder, Ignatius of Loyola. At least it should be. As I've noted in chapter 1, his wisdom lies hidden in several documents—in his spiritual journal, or *Autobiography*; in the *Constitutions* he wrote for his followers; and in the retreat outline written from personal experience and known as the *Spiritual Exercises*, which should not be separated from the *Directory* he intended for the use of the experienced guide who assists the person making the Exercises.

Discernment and the search for God's will are the warp and woof of Ignatian spirituality, but the Ignatian way of discernment cannot be learned from books. It can only be experienced under the direction of a sensitive guide. Such guides are available on Jesuit university campuses, typically through retreat programs, to work with people interested in making the Spiritual Exercises. A special task, a privileged opportunity, for Jesuits in higher education is to open the book of the Spiritual Exercises to those who want to grow spiritually. In this context, as in the classroom, learning is directed by a motivator-organizer and assimilated by an active participant in the process. In the retreat experience, one learns how to pray. In the classroom experience, one learns how to learn. As classroom educator or spiritual guide, the Jesuit tries, as an instrument of God's grace, to assist the Spirit in moving the minds and hearts of those who want to grow.

In the domain of higher education, there are many (students, faculty, and staff alike) with the potential for wisdom. That is why Jesuits gather at colleges and universities to work. Their task is not only to teach and search for truth in all its forms but also to share their founder's special grace with those who want to grow in the Ignatian way. Often on Jesuit campuses there can be found a Jesuit whose assignment is to explain the Ignatian heritage and to bring interested members of faculty, staff, or student body into closer experiential contact with this spiritual tradition.

Christian wisdom is to "know you, the only true God, and the one whom you sent, Jesus Christ" (John 17:3). There is an Ignatian way toward this wisdom. It is Ignatian, not Jesuit in any proprietary sense; hence it is there to be shared with others. The Jesuit is expected to have internalized this way. His educational methods will, not surprisingly, reflect it. His normal desire will be to live and work in companionship with others who know this way, so he lives in community with other Jesuits. And his hope will be to share this way or see it shared with others. This is all part of the Jesuit purpose in higher education or in any other work.

The Jesuit, by vocation, is trained "to seek God in all things," even in quite secular and esoteric things and in academically rarefied surroundings. Seeking and finding God in all things is a bedrock Jesuit principle. And on this bedrock rests the traditional Jesuit commitment, in theory and in practice, to a Catholic Christian humanism. God is in all things human.

Not all Jesuits are skilled in sharing their Ignatian spirituality with lay colleagues. But few would not attach high importance to the sharing. And all support the various mechanisms in place within or around Jesuit institutions to facilitate this sharing. The realization of all these ideals, the translation of this theory into practice, is a personal challenge to Jesuit fidelity. The Society of Jesus lives on the trust it places in each of its members to appropriate the essentials of its spiritual heritage, to sustain them in himself by God's grace, and to pass them on to others who want to grow in this way.

A brochure inviting prospective students—the kind who want to grow—to consider enrolling at the Jesuit-run University of Scranton states the matter simply and well:

> College is an integral part of life's journey. Over the next four years, you'll gain knowledge, acquire skills and forge relationships that will last a lifetime. At the University of Scranton, we offer a liberal arts education in the dual Jesuit traditions of *cura personalis*—care for the whole person— and the *magis*—a restless pursuit of excellence. In this remarkable community of inquiry, as scholars and learners together, you'll develop healthy habits of the mind and heart that will serve you well in any endeavor you choose.

That's another way of explaining why Jesuits are in higher education.

Learn, Lead, and Serve

At Loyola College in Maryland, the educational mission is specified as enabling students to "learn, lead, and serve in a diverse and challenging world." This is a traditional and characteristically Jesuit ambition. It is reasonable to assume that maturing persons are attracted to higher education communities as students precisely because they want to grow. True, when they arrive as freshmen, they are only four years out of the eighth grade. But they will mature a lot over their four years with us. It is no less reasonable to assume that Jesuits (and their like-minded lay colleagues) will want to meet them there in order to assist, in the Ignatian way, in the development of such great human potential.

Time will test the reasonableness of both assumptions (that those interested in growth will come and that Jesuits and lay colleagues interested in facilitating that growth will be there to meet them). Faith will enable the Jesuits now in higher education to face up to the test of time, for only time can tell whether their ranks will increase, be depleted, or remain just about the same. Meanwhile, college- and university-based Jesuits have before them the twin challenge of excelling in the discovery and communication of truth while sharing their spiritual heritage with those, especially lay colleagues, who want it. The task is theirs (the Jesuits'), but the power to realize the hoped-for outcome is the Lord's.

In recent decades, as we shall see in subsequent chapters, Jesuits have come to see their role in education as forming men and women for others. Education for justice is a central concern. The service of faith and the promotion of justice now constitute the twin goals of any authentic Jesuit work. This is what we do. This is our reason for existence in the contemporary world. And this, to make the point explicit, is the aim of the Jesuit effort in educating young men and women for careers in business and other secular pursuits.

It is natural and most appropriate, in the Jesuit way of proceeding, to indicate that there is a connection, a genuine relevance, between religious faith and the world of work. It is not our purpose to convert students or colleagues to the Catholic faith, although we want them all to know we believe that a genuine faith commitment is important for a full human life and that anyone's faith commitment is worthy of respect. This point of view is one of the distinctive strengths that sets our professional schools apart.

The familiar Jesuit motto—*ad majorem Dei gloriam*, "For the greater glory of God"—imbues Jesuits and their works with a restlessness, a drive, a proper ambition. It is no admission of illness to declare a hope to get better; it is no sign of weakness to admit that there is room for improvement. Education, by definition, invites participants on both sides of the teaching-learning transaction to get better, to improve, to move forward. Jesuit business education today, along with the broader Jesuit educational effort, is moving forward in a great tradition, a tradition that helps explain the purpose of the entire enterprise.

Reason and Spirit

Some would describe this tradition in one word: the *magis*. Let me close with a reflection on why I think spirituality is getting a lot of attention these days. There is a lot of searching going on in the hearts of men and women who are concerned about the relevance of their religious faith to their workplace responsibilities. I think something has been troubling the American psyche for the past sixty years that is prompting us now to focus on spirituality, and I think Jesuit schools are meeting this need across the board in all our departments, majors, and centers. I have to go back to the end of World War II to identify what I think is happening in the American mind and in our broader culture. In doing this, I find it helpful to point the reader to the opening of my book on workplace spirituality, *Answers from Within: Spiritual Guidelines for Managing Setbacks in Work and Life.*[2] Let me summarize those remarks here.

More than six decades ago, *Time* magazine ran a cover story about an event that shook the world, an event that wounded us so profoundly that it has remained to trouble us, mind and soul, ever since. The incident, which was reported in the August 20, 1945, issue of the magazine, marked both an end and a beginning.

This report was published, as were all *Time* stories in those days, without attribution of authorship. I learned years later that a young (and then relatively unknown) *Time* staffer by the name of James Agee wrote the piece under a very tight deadline. The overarching headline was "Victory." The first subhead was "The Peace." The second subhead was "The Bomb."

Time was covering a big story that week, perhaps the biggest of our century. Agee saw the "controlled splitting of the atom," which produced the bomb used to attack Hiroshima and Nagasaki and thus brought to an end the greatest conflict in human history, as an event so enormous that in comparison "the war itself shrank to minor significance." To Agee's eye, "Humanity, already profoundly perplexed and disunified, was brought inescapably into a new age in which all thoughts and things were split—and far from controlled."

Time's readers, still dizzy with the thrill of victory, could hardly have seen, as Agee did, the potential for both good and evil that the atomic bomb represented. That potential bordered, he said, "on the infinite—with this further, terrible split in the fact: that upon a people already so nearly drowned in materialism even in peacetime, the good uses of this power might easily bring disaster as prodigious as the evil." Then Agee made a shattering observation that rings every bit as true today as it did that memorable August. Here are the words he wrote—words that were available to any reader of the nation's most popular newsmagazine in 1945 and that have gone largely unheeded these many years since: "Man's fate has forever been shaped between the hands of reason and spirit, now in collaboration, again in conflict. Now reason and spirit meet on final ground. If either or anything is to survive, they must find a way to create an indissoluble partnership."

These powerful words were perceptive and prophetic. They appeared just before the so-called baby boomers were born. They explain, I think, the cause of the split that has been troubling us for so long. We have not yet forged the "indissoluble partnership" between reason and spirit; we are even more adrift now than we were then on a sea of materialism. We may, however, be beginning to notice what Agee saw when the bomb split open the universe, namely, that each of us is responsible for his or her own soul.

Men and women in the world of work who are restless and wondering about the relevance of their Sunday faith to their Monday responsibilities are, I believe, being nudged now by the Spirit, the Holy Spirit, to begin an exploration into God. Working this theme into what we Jesuits and our lay colleagues do in the classroom is yet another indication that we have something distinctive, something to offer that clearly sets us apart from other schools and other educators. If you are curious enough to inquire about who is going to do this in the future, you find all the tea leaves predicting that, if it is to be done at all, it can only be done by laymen and laywomen.

In the fall of 1998, Loyola College in Maryland produced a document that includes this memorable statement about Jesuit education:

> In 1599, the Spanish Jesuit Diego Ledesma listed four reasons why the Society of Jesus involved itself in education: (1) to give students "advantages for practical living"; (2) to "contribute to the right government of public affairs"; (3) to "give ornament, splendor, and perfection to the rational nature" of humanity; (4) to be a "bulwark of religion and guide man most surely and easily to the achievement of his last end." Ledesma's definition focuses clearly on what Jesuit education hopes for in its students, and any mission statement faithful to the Jesuit spirit must keep students and our responsibility to them at its center. With a bit of "translation" into late twentieth-century American terms, Ledesma's words still point clearly to key distinguishing characteristics of a Jesuit education: (1) it is eminently practical, focused on providing students with the knowledge and skills to excel in whatever field they choose; (2) it is not merely practical, but concerns itself also with

questions of values, with educating men and women to be good citizens and good leaders, concerned with the common good, and able to use their education for the service of faith and promotion of justice; (3) it celebrates the full range of human intellectual power and achievement, confidently affirming reason, not as antithetical to faith, but as its necessary complement; (4) it places all that it does firmly within a Christian understanding of the human person as a creature of God whose ultimate destiny is beyond the human. To put these goals in the words of the Decrees of the 34th General Congregation, Jesuit education encourages students and their teachers alike not only to seek knowledge for its own sake, but also to ask continually the key question, "Knowledge for what?" It also insists that answers to that question be formed in the context of vigorous intellectual activity that excludes no evidence from the investigation, including the evidence of the deposit of Christian faith.

Just as Willie Sutton once explained that he robbed banks "because that's where the money is," Jesuits and their lay colleagues in colleges and universities might say that they are in higher education because that is where ambitious goals can be both set and met for the discovery of truth and the development of human potential. It is more to them than just a career. It is a call to reach new heights for the glory of God and the service of their fellows in the human community.

CHAPTER 3

Why We Are in Secondary Education

Suppose that I ruled the world of Catholic education from kindergarten through graduate school and—to let the imagination roam for a moment and serve up this challenging hypothetical—that I were pushed up against a wall of choice and told I could have only four years under explicitly Catholic auspices. Fortunately, Catholic education in the U.S. does not have to make that tough choice, but if it did, and if the choice were mine, I'd choose the high school years.

I'm convinced that the potential for a positive educational impact is greater in the secondary school years than in any other four-year block of time allocated to the formal educational process and that this is why the Jesuits have been in secondary education ("colleges," as they were called in Europe) almost from the beginning. There is something special about those years between elementary school and college. Why?

To explain my bias in this regard, I have to go back to what I call the "center of significance" and let it make an analytical point. The newborn child constitutes the center of significance in his or her unfolding life. All experiences, all surrounding influences—heat or cold, hunger or satisfaction, pleasure or pain, comfort or discomfort—are measured by the infant in reference to the self. Self constitutes the center of significance in the infant's life. The self-centered reference remains fixed through many months of being held, fed, changed, and bathed, and it is reinforced by tactile and vocal attention provided by significant others.

As both the presence and awareness of siblings and peers enter the world of the developing child, parents move into the center of significance in that child's life. Parents become the point of reference for what the child begins to value, how the child begins to walk and talk, where the child goes, and who the child knows. Parents can expect to hold this spotlight position in the child's life for about a decade. At some point in the pre- or early adolescent years of the developing youngster's life, it becomes clear that the parents no longer hold the central reference position. They no longer constitute the center of significance for the child. The center, however, is never vacant for long. Friends and peers—"the gang," "my group"—can now take center stage. Peer pressure can push anchorless youngsters into a forced march of adolescent conformity, or the center can be filled with a hero from the world of sports or entertainment. It can be filled by an older brother or sister, a friend, a neighbor, an uncle, or an aunt. It can be filled by the child him- or herself, thus signaling a reversion to infantile self-centeredness. It can also be filled by a significant adult in the school setting—a teacher, coach, or counselor.

In the process of development, there is a natural and inevitable separation from parents. At some point in the early teen years, there should be a natural, but by no means inevitable, reconnection with parents. The reconnection must not be a forged manacle of parental domination and infantile dependency. Ideally, it should be mediated by a subsequent occupant of the privileged position that I've been referring to here as the center of significance. The reconnection should be forged in terms of new humanistic links and revised caring relationships involving parents and their teenage offspring. Parents choose to have children; they do not, however, choose the unique child person and personality who is related to them as daughter or son.

Parent-Child Reconnection

Children do not choose their birth parents. But as young adults, they can decide to do just that. I certainly think they should. And so should parents choose their teenage children. This is the meaning of reconnection. Teenagers and parents should choose one another, choose to relate to one another in perfectly appropriate ways for persons of separate identity, unique personality, and relative independence.

In my view, the Jesuit high school is especially well suited to mediating this process of reconnection. It is a natural role for the high school professional, and that is one of the reasons why Jesuits choose to work in that setting. It is not, of course, the only reason; their tradition puts them there. As John C. Olin comments in *The Autobiography of St. Ignatius Loyola*, "This first activity (teaching Christian doctrine every day to children) at Azpeitia (in 1535) became one of the primary purposes of the Society of Jesus when it was organized in 1539–40."[1] Olin opines that Ignatius would agree with Erasmus, who, defending such instruction, argued "that Christ did not despise the very young, and that no age of man was more deserving of generous help, and nowhere could a richer harvest be anticipated, since the young are the growing crop and growing timber of the commonwealth."

The Jesuit high school also is quite likely to provide a positive peer-group environment for the developing adolescent, and that is one of the many reasons why parents choose to put their children in that setting. At an informal interprovince Jesuit gathering one summer, I noticed a priest wearing a blue T-shirt with these words printed in white on the back: "Educating men of competence, conscience, and compassion in the Jesuit tradition since 1872. AMDG." The wearer has been working *ad majorem Dei gloriam* for many years as a teacher at a school whose name appeared elsewhere on the shirt: St. Peter's Prep in Jersey City, New Jersey.

Campion High School (a Jesuit boarding school that closed its doors in the 1960s) in Prairie du Chien, Wisconsin, had this motto on its official letterhead: "Send us a boy, and we'll give you back a man." Students playfully added the letters *iac* to the last word in that motto, but many loyal alumni, particularly in the Chicago area, sing the praises of that great school.

Another Jesuit high school that closed about twenty years ago is Brooklyn Prep. On an August afternoon in 1998, I found myself in the company of Bob Bennett, a famous Washington lawyer, on the four o'clock US Airways shuttle from New York to Washington. We were detained on the ground at LaGuardia Airport because of storm systems to the west. LaGuardia soon became like a crowded parking lot. Along with a virtual fleet of other planes, we were on the tarmac for four hours before being cleared for takeoff, so Bob Bennett and I had plenty of time to talk. He wanted to talk about Brooklyn Prep.

"I'm fifty-nine years old," he said, "and I still have vivid memories of my high school years. After graduating from Brooklyn Prep, I studied at Georgetown, the University of Virginia, and Harvard. Without any doubt at all, I'd say that the best education I received—by far—happened in those four years at Brooklyn Prep." He went on to name Jesuits who had a major impact on his life back then (one of whom he remains quite close to and considers a valued friend). "I cross-examined a thousand witnesses long before I ever went to law school," said Bob Bennett. "I did it as a high school debater at Brooklyn Prep."

Thousands of Brooklyn Prep alumni still meet for annual reunions and communion breakfasts; they contribute annually to a scholarship fund for the education of economically disadvantaged youngsters.

We also spoke about Bob Bennett's famous younger brother Bill, who, because the family had moved to Washington, attended Gonzaga High School just a few blocks from the Capitol. Bill Bennett later went to Williams College with the encouragement of his Gonzaga headmaster, Jesuit Father Tony McHale. By Bill's account, Father McHale said to this competitive, opinionated, and argumentative young man during his senior year, "Bennett, you shouldn't go to a Catholic college; enroll someplace where they will rough you up intellectually and challenge your faith." Bill Bennett, with a doctorate in philosophy from the University of Texas, later ran the National Humanities Center in North Carolina and the National Endowment for the Humanities in Washington and served as President Reagan's secretary of education. Never omitted from his official résumé was the fact that he graduated from Gonzaga High School. This was younger brother Bennett's way of acknowledging what he considered to be a personal debt and giving credit to the place that opened up the world of classical literature for him.

The Califano Experience

Another famous lawyer, Joseph A. Califano Jr., a 1948 graduate of Brooklyn Prep, was secretary of health, education, and welfare in the Carter administration; he now runs the Center on Addiction and Substance Abuse at Columbia University. Some years ago, he gave the keynote address to an assembly of Jesuit secondary school educators from the Jesuits' New York Province (which has seven of the forty-five Jesuit high schools in the country).

Califano began by saying, "I came here today because I think you are doing the most important work of our society. The adolescent years are the most formative in our culture, and today's high school students face monumental challenges. If you can make it with adolescents, you are making it in the toughest human turf in modern day America. For your commitment, I salute you. Stick with it. You are indeed the best hope of the next generation, and they need all the energy, commitment, and devotion you can muster in them." He continued:

The Jesuits at Brooklyn Prep had a powerful influence on me. In immediate terms it was their encouragement that led me to go to Holy Cross College (where, in addition to getting a fine education, I also was urged to go to Harvard Law School). At Harvard, three of us "Crusaders" from Holy Cross, Jesuit high school graduates from, respectively, St. Peter's in Jersey City, N.J., Brooklyn Prep, and Regis [High School in New York City], graduated first, third, and fifth in the 1955 Law School class of 525.

For the long run, the Prep whetted my intellectual appetite, particularly through its courses in literature, religion and history. We were exposed to the grace of English poetry, to Shakespeare's tragedies and comedies, to carefully selected American literature. . . . We studied American and English history—though we called it world history at the time.

The Jesuits at Brooklyn Prep put flesh on the bones of the moral values my parents had given me. And this came not so much in the classroom as in the extracurricular activities, conversations with teachers after class, work on the school newspaper, and the school's interest in current events. I don't want to overstate this. I was a typical fun-loving, partying, cigarette-smoking and, in my senior year, beer-drinking adolescent. But there had also been implanted the seeds of the skills that would enable me to get the most out of Holy Cross and its philosophy and ethics courses—in those days, all Holy Cross students majored in philosophy—and to absorb the more progressive values available at Harvard Law School and to handle that school's heavy work load.

Also planted were the seeds of discipline, especially intellectual discipline and study habits, which were so valuable in law school and later in life. And I must credit the Jesuits with starting the process of teaching me how to think. They imbued me with a healthy skepticism and taught me the importance of never letting it descend into cynicism.

The reader will wonder whether this experience is still available in today's Jesuit high school. Much has changed, but there is still a language-based curriculum, although it allows for more exposure to art and music than the Califano generation and its predecessors enjoyed. There is also more and better laboratory-based science, including computer science, along with mathematics advanced far beyond the pre-space age boundaries of even the better prep schools. In a recent year, according to the Jesuit Secondary Education Association, 86 percent of Jesuit prep school students took four or more years of English; 87 percent took three or more years of a foreign language; 80 percent took four or more years of mathematics, with 32 percent studying calculus. In addition, 86 percent of these students took three or more years of natural sciences, and 89 percent took three or more years of social sciences. Community-service projects are an integral part of the curriculum; they extend the students' reach to inner-city neighborhoods, rural areas, and even foreign countries.

There are fewer Jesuits but more extracurricular activities and many more laymen and laywomen to have character-forming conversations with the young. Here is Mr. Califano's advice to all of them—lay and Jesuit—who are involved in this work:

> First, accept the unique importance of your work. Adolescence is where it's at. There are no more important formative years than the years young men and women spend with you. . . .
>
> Second, in a society as wide-open and drenched in get-it-now materialism as ours is, the most important seeds you can plant are those that teach your students how to make choices. Most of your students can be just about anything they want to be, do just about anything they want to do, and indulge in any pleasure they wish. It is essential that you imbue these students with standards and values that will help them make choices about everything from

the entertainments they watch and participate in to the colleges they attend and the careers they pursue.

Third, you must help young Americans understand the importance of being effective citizens. The key here is the recognition that in an effective citizen knowledge and involvement are locked together. Knowledge without engagement is the stuff of impotence, and engagement without knowledge is the stuff of demagoguery.

You will find the Jesuit way of making choices outlined in considerable detail in chapter 6. Jesuit spirituality is a spirituality of choice, and it is natural for Jesuits to be both noncoercive and nondirective in assisting the young with their decision-making challenges without in any way just leaving the decision maker to his or her own inexperience, fears, and impulses.

Very early in the 1996–97 academic year at Georgetown University, Brendan Hurley, one of the young Jesuits on the campus-ministry team, invited about one hundred freshmen, who came to Georgetown from Jesuit high schools all across the country, to gather one evening around nine in the Jesuit Community dining room for pizza and conversation about their shared experience of Jesuit secondary education. The hope was to facilitate a certain bonding and to open up opportunities for these young men and women to carry over into the college years some of the characteristic Jesuit values they acquired in high school. Remarkably, the secondary school experience that had the greatest impact on the largest number of those young alumni was what the high schools call the Kairos Retreat—several days, often a weekend away, spent in prayer, reflection, and discussion about faith, values, and the future. All the Jesuit high schools have them. Parents are asked to provide a letter, written from the heart, that will be given to the youngster toward the end of the retreat. *Kairos* is an anglicization of the Greek word meaning "the right moment," "a decision point," "a time for action." Students remember the retreat that way, often as a defining moment. They also remember an experience of affirmation, a sense of being loved by the parents who wrote to them and by the God who became present to them in a new way during the retreat.

The Latin expression *eloquentia perfecta* has for centuries been associated with the stated goals of Jesuit education, particularly secondary education as it evolved in the United States. Debates, dramatics, public-speaking competitions, oral presentations in class, daily written work in varying forms and in several languages, journalistic and editorial tasks on school newspapers, literary quarterlies, and yearbooks—all of these are a familiar part of Jesuit secondary education. Even in this "age of the image" and in the boundaryless world of cyberspace, the Jesuit high school student meets schoolmasters and activity moderators every day who impress upon their charges the importance of the spoken and written word. Using words well on paper or aloud is a special goal of Jesuit education. And how could it be otherwise? If education of leaders (Jesuit schools are clear about having that as a mission) is to be effective, it begins with an acknowledgment that the world moves on words and numbers. Literacy and numeracy belong in the tool kit of the leader. Without them, the would-be leader will not simply fall behind; he or she won't even know where the parade of human progress is headed!

New Initiatives

Although some Jesuit secondary schools have closed in the U.S. in recent decades, others have opened. In Chicago, for example, Cristo del Rey Jesuit High School was founded in 1996 for the immigrant Hispanic population of the Pilsen/Little Village neighborhood. Cristo Rey is a coeducational school that offers classes taught in both English and Spanish. The curriculum combines traditional Jesuit college-preparatory education with a work-study program that provides the students with entry-level positions in Chicago corporations while they are going to school. This is what the colleges call "cooperative education," enabling students to earn enough to pay their tuition at school and learn enough on the job to gain a leg up on permanent full-time employment when formal schooling is over.

In the early 1980s, Father Malcolm Carron, SJ, stepped down after many years as president of the University of Detroit to become president of the financially troubled University of Detroit High School. From that position and vantage point, he was able to appreciate what his provincial, Father Joseph Daoust, and officials of the Archdiocese of Detroit had already seen, namely, the need for a pre-prep school to serve some of that city's economically impoverished African American boys. So, with financing from both the province and the archdiocese, Father Carron became the first president of Loyola Academy for sixth, seventh, and eighth graders. What to the secular, prestige-influenced, and career-focused eye would appear to be downward social and occupational mobility, appeared to this apostolic Jesuit a great opportunity to do what Jesuits have done from their earliest days—serve the poor and educate future leaders. This 1993 academy initiative evolved into a new high school, known now as Loyola High School, that is dedicated to the service of poor African American boys.

Another new Jesuit educational initiative began in Baltimore in 1993. Readers of George F. Will's syndicated newspaper column learned about it four years after it was up and running. Here is an excerpt from George Will's op-ed article "Micro-Solutions to Macro-Problems."[2]

> They come from nineteen zip codes, some leaving home before 6 a.m., some taking three buses. They head for home at 5:15 p.m. with several hours of homework ahead.
>
> The boys (forty-nine African Americans, two Africans, four Hispanic Americans, three Caucasians) at this inner-city middle school, now four years old, that offers grades six, seven, and eight, begin their day with a ritual of civility. They shake hands with their thirty-one-year-old headmaster, Jeff

Sindler, and with the Rev. William Watters, SJ, sixty-two, and with any other adult in the vestibule, looking each in the eye and saying, "Good morning." Poor enunciation is corrected.

✳ *Eloquentia perfecta* is an important consideration at the beginning of every school day at St. Ignatius Loyola Academy, the apostolic creation of Father Watters, veteran pastor of the Baltimore landmark St. Ignatius Church. George Will heard about the school and called Father Watters to request permission to spend a day there.

His column begins by establishing that "it is 7:15 a.m., dark, cold, and drizzling when, from the sidewalk in front of the winding stone steps that lead to the door . . . the noisiness begins." After the handshake and good-morning greeting, the school day starts. Let George Will show you around.

> After demolishing—but with table manners monitored— stacks of waffles, two-thirds of the boys clean the school with mops and vacuum cleaners. The other third practice public speaking. "Ebonics"—the patois of America's meanest streets—is not spoken here. This day the boys take turns reading from newsmagazines. After each finishes, the teacher invites comments from the others, "supportive" comments first ("great eye contact," "good level pace"), then "constructive" criticism.

Will repeats the technical language used to describe the academy's student body ("adjudicated and at-risk youths"). He describes the socioeconomic background of the students and is pleased that "they all come dressed neatly in the school uniform (white or blue shirt, dark tie, dark slacks, no sneakers, no exceptions)." The boys are always addressed as "gentlemen." When they graduate from their completely subsidized (by voluntary contributions) academy, they go on, with scholarship support, to some of Baltimore's best private schools. I'm surprised that the columnist made no mention of the fact that all students in the academy take three years of Latin. One that I know of, now a freshman scholarship student at Georgetown Prep, continues to study Latin and intends to take Greek.

"What is the significance of Loyola's little swarm of fifty-eight boys in the larger scheme of things?" asks Will. "Just this: Enough micro-solutions and there will be no macro-problems." The writer concludes his column by noting that "the handbook says the school aims to impart to students a desire to be 'competent men for others.'" Will then adds, "If the language strikes contemporary sensibilities as stilted, and as a faint quaint echo from another century, so much the worse for ours."

Values from another century, the sixteenth century of Ignatius of Loyola, are indeed alive and well in an impressive range of Jesuit secondary and middle schools that offer macro-hopes along with school-based solutions to this century's problems. No wonder Jesuits and their lay colleagues want to spend their working lives there.

CHAPTER 4

Education for Social Justice

This chapter did not appear in the original edition of *Jesuit Saturdays*; it is added here because of the need to make explicit the important contribution Jesuit schools and colleges can make to the contemporary mission of the Society of Jesus, namely, the service of faith and promotion of justice.

The Society's Thirty-Fifth General Congregation, held in 2008 to elect a new superior general, took the occasion to reaffirm the emphasis previous General Congregations (particularly GC 32, 1974–75, Decree 4), put on the justice dimension of Jesuit ministry. It would be a great mistake, in my view, for Jesuits to walk away from their schools in the misguided belief that the schools are not useful instruments in the all-important mission of assisting the poor and promoting justice.

Direct ministry to the poor and creative new approaches to promoting justice will surely be necessary, but instruments already in hand, namely, the schools, colleges, universities, and research centers have great potential for participation in the worldwide Jesuit effort to build a better—read, more just—world.

To put a Christian perspective on education for justice is a structural approach, not a simple adjustment in the angle of vision. To specify social justice, not justice alone, as an educational objective is also a structural specification. I will discuss each of these points separately, inviting the reader to ponder the implications of what follows for the educational institutions, secondary and higher, that carry the Jesuit brand name.

First, what new reality is involved in a Christian approach to justice? Second, how does social justice differ from interpersonal justice and what, if any, are the implications of this difference for those who would attempt to educate for social justice?

In considering all that follows, the reader might consider as well an etymological suggestion. Issues of social justice are structural concerns. Would not etymology suggest that instruction, normally associated with education, might have some important relationship to the construction or reconstruction of the social order?

For the Jewish contemporaries of Jesus, the Kingdom of God connoted the realization of the ideal of a just ruler. As Walter Kasper puts it in *Jesus the Christ* (Burns & Oates, 1976), "in the ancient Middle Eastern conception, justice did not consist primarily in impartial judgments, but in help and protection for the helpless, weak, and poor. The coming of the Kingdom of God was expected to be the liberation from unjust rule and the establishment of the justice of God in the world."

The Kingdom of God Is at Hand

In that context and to those contemporaries, Jesus proclaimed his message, "The Kingdom of God is at hand" (Mark 1:15). He added to that proclamation the instruction to "repent" and to "believe the gospel." Hence, a response to his proclamation required both faith and an attitudinal change, a *metanoia*. Something new, some hoped-for relief from unjust and exploitative rule was, with the arrival of Jesus in human history, "at hand." Something new, some change of heart on the part of those who received the proclamation would be required to permit that which was "at hand" to be accepted, to take hold.

Those whose work is Jesuit education are laboring for the establishment of that same Kingdom of God, a kingdom of justice and peace, a kingdom that is still at hand but not yet grasped, not yet fully realized. Presumably, those who teach in Jesuit schools will want to explain these justice themes in class—theology, sociology, literature—and encourage the application of these themes in out-of-class activities, especially community service.

Jesuit education is a ministry of the Church. It is in and of the Church, a Church which is a community, a pilgrim people, on the way to kingdom. It is important to understand the meaning of the term *kingdom* as Jesus used it. It is not a place. Rudolf Schnackenburg in *God's Rule and the Kingdom* (Herder and Herder, 1963) insists that it is a rule, a reign, a leadership . . . which develops from Yahweh's absolute power and shows itself in the guidance of Israel. This original meaning, that Yahweh as king actively "rules," must be kept in mind through the whole growth of the kingdom theme. God's kingship in the Bible is not characterized by latent authority, but by the exercise of power, not by an office but a function, it is not a title, but a deed. Jesus proclaimed himself to be the doer of that deed, the holder of that power. Kingdom is an exercise of power. The power to establish justice is the Lord's. The task to work for justice is ours. And the pity of it all is the fact that the power indeed is "at hand" and has been at hand for two thousand years, but the egalitarian characteristics of the kingdom have not yet taken hold because the response to the proclamation has, to date, carried with it an insufficient change of heart, an insufficient attitudinal change, an unwillingness on the part of those who "have" to "let go" for the benefit of those who are deprived.

Jesus' own preaching of the kingdom destroys our own closely held preconceptions; it challenges the hearer toward value reversal. The poor, not the rich, are "blessed" he says (Matthew 5:3); the persecuted, not the comfortable, are "blessed" as well (Matthew 5:10). As John R. Donahue, SJ, has commented, there are very direct social implications in the kingdom proclamation because Jesus shatters the social conventions of his time by making, as the sign of the arrival of the kingdom, his fellowship with the outcasts of society. The teaching of Jesus reveals a very clear preference for the poor. He displays what might be called a compensatory bias, a characteristic impulse to use his power to empower the powerless. He tries to move, by example, by persuasion, and by threat of damnation, the heart of the unjust oppressor in order to bring relief to the victim of oppression. There is no "unrightable wrong" in the face of his person and power. There are only resistant hearts and closed minds in the face of his gospel proclamation.

But what is new or different in a Christian or specifically Jesuit approach to justice? What did Jesus add to earlier understandings of justice? To answer this it is necessary to consider justice as Jesus taught it. This is particularly important for Christian educators who are called, as the title of the American Bishops' 1972 Pastoral on Catholic Education puts it, "To Teach As Jesus Did." Justice, as Jesus taught it, is something different from the justice of Plato and Aristotle.

It is my view that education for justice must be, in some recognizable form, Christian (and therefore Jesuit) education. To the extent that this sounds outrageously arrogant, it measures with accuracy the sinfulness, the social sinfulness, of the Christian people. It also measures the distance between the contemporary Christian community (of which Jesuits and their learning communities are a part) and the kingdom which was announced, two thousand years ago, to be "at hand."

There is continuity, not discontinuity, between Old Testament and New. The continuity resides in the person and teaching of Jesus. In tracing the continuity from Old Testament origins to New Testament specifications, I begin with a famous text from the Book of Micah: "What is good has been explained to you, man; this is what Yahweh asks of you: only this, to act justly, to love tenderly and to walk humbly with your God" (Micah 6:8 JB). Justice, as Jesus taught it, involved a conscious and explicit integration of those two ideas, "to act justly," and "to love tenderly." Cold, impartial "treating-equals-equally" or "to everyone his or her due" understandings of justice fall short of the mark set by Jesus for the Christian. From either a personal or social perspective, the root problems he set out to correct, it seems to me, are all reducible to powerlessness, poverty, and indignity. The means he chose to employ in correcting them were educational.

He taught by word and example the unity of justice and love. "To act justly," according to the example and teaching of Jesus, meant also "to love tenderly." Love without justice is not Christian love. Justice without love is not Christian justice. Where do I find this New Testament specification? The late Fordham theologian Charles H. Giblin, SJ, suggested in a lecture some years ago that Luke 15 presents justice in a new way, in the context of mercy and love. That particular chapter in Luke contains three parables on God's mercy. They were addressed to the Pharisees and the scribes who complained, says Luke, because "The tax collectors and the sinners . . . were all seeking his company to hear what he had to say" (Luke 15:1 JB). The most famous of those three parables, directed in Luke's grouping toward the scribes and the Pharisees, is the story of the prodigal son. But as Father Giblin observed, it is the dialogue with the elder son that reveals an underdeveloped notion of justice, an unawareness of the necessary integration of justice with love. The dutiful ("every man his due") elder son will have to change his notion of justice in order to enter into the celebration. If he chooses not to change, he may not go into the house. He must "repent," undergo a *metanoia*, if he is to accept the new understanding that is there "at hand."

Justice as Jesus Taught It

In the tenth chapter of St. Luke another duty-obligation story makes the same point, but much more dramatically. It is the parable of the Good Samaritan. First there is the question, "What must I do to inherit eternal life?" In reply, Jesus repeats the Old Testament instruction to love your neighbor "as yourself." Then the lawyer who had posed the prior question asks, "And who is my neighbor?" The reply this time is a parable about an abandoned victim of a roadside beating and robbery. Along in close succession come a dutiful priest and a dutiful Levite who see the victim but pass him by. Their sense of duty did not move them to assist the man. According to their assessment, apparently, duty required no action of them in that particular situation. "But a Samaritan traveler who came upon him was moved with compassion when he saw him." Compassion enters the instruction, and through the instruction compassion, mercy, and love enter the structure of a Christian response to powerlessness, poverty, and indignity. The rest of the parable further elaborates the notion of justice as Jesus taught it.

This, it seems to me, is a specifically Christian development. It is a development of, not discontinuous with, the Old Testament teaching. Consider Hosea:

> And I will betroth you to myself for ever,
> betroth you with integrity and justice,
> with tenderness and love. (Hosea 2:21 JB)

All the elements are there in Hosea. They are specifically integrated in the person and teaching of Jesus. Consider Amos proclaiming the Lord's preference for right over rite:

> I reject your oblations,
> and refuse to look at your sacrifices of fattened cattle.
> Let me have no more of the din of your chanting,
> no more of your strumming on harps.
> But let justice flow like water,
> and integrity like an unfailing stream. (Amos 5:22–24 JB)

As Shalom Spiegel points out, the very word that Amos used, *sedaqah*, came to mean in later times "justice made clairvoyant by love, i.e., charity."

The "startling and distinctive note in the Christian message," according to Johannes Metz, is the idea that the love of neighbor is not something different from the love of God; "it is merely the earthly side of the same coin." Similarly, the startling and distinctive note in the Christian view of justice is the conscious and explicit integration of justice with love. The beaten and robbed traveler, the oppressed, deprived, and subjugated human person is also, as a result of the Incarnation of Jesus, the image of God himself. In our encounters with such persons, we encounter God. When we pass such a person by, we pass by our God. "Our human brother now becomes a 'sacrament' of God's hidden presence among us, a mediator between God and man." Such is Metz's expression of the Christian view.

So much for my first point concerning the new reality involved in a Christian approach to justice. It remains now to explore the differences between social and interpersonal or individual justice, and to examine the implications of those differences for those who would educate for social justice.

"As He died to make men holy let us die to make men free," is a solemn and familiar line from the "Battle Hymn of the Republic." Many prefer to substitute "live" for "die" as they sing those words. This is one way of stating the dramatic challenge confronting the Christian in quest of social justice. Let Christians, in their various social groupings, live in a way that promotes freedom for those in other social groupings. Such living will reflect the values of Him who died to make us holy. One such value is justice integrated with love.

In considering social justice, I have in mind group-to-group relationships. Hence, relatedness between the groups must be presupposed before one group may be said to have a justice relationship to another group. I find it helpful to use the framework of the traditional symbolism of the scales of justice to look for relatedness in situations of social injustice. Social injustice affects a group, a disadvantaged group occupying the up tray on the imbalanced scale. What group occupies the down tray? In matters of social injustice, the occupants of the counterpart down tray will normally have to "let go," give something up, before the trays can be brought into balance. And balance, of course, symbolizes a condition of justice between the groups.

Social justice includes both legal justice (which intends the common good) and distributive justice (which intends the good of each individual as a member of the group), but social justice focuses not on legal rights and obligations but rather on the natural rights and obligations *of the group* in relationship to other groups.

It is a mistake, in my view, to label certain one-to-one relationships as relationships of social justice simply because the disadvantaged beneficiary of that particular exchange is poor or identified with an oppressed minority group. A helping or saving initiative from the advantaged individual to the disadvantaged individual may, indeed, be not only an act of charity but an instance of justice as Jesus taught it. Recall the Good Samaritan. But it is not necessarily helpful to the group—either group, the helping or the helped. Hence, it is not really an instance of social justice. If the repentance, the change of heart, the *metanoia* does not touch the group which takes its advantage at the expense of the other group (that is precisely what relatedness may imply), then the structural support for the imbalance will be neither weakened nor changed.

Similarly, if a person-to-group initiative (say, an individual landlord to an entire neighborhood) benefits the disadvantaged neighborhood group without moving others in the advantaged group toward structural change, this falls short, in my view, of a social justice relationship because there is no social group (in this case, say, a board of realtors) on one side of the initiative. It is difficult these days to get people into groups to do things together! All the more difficult is it to get groups to take justice initiatives toward other groups.

Understanding Social Justice

Social justice looks to all members of the group. In a context of obligation, social justice looks for a group initiative, a group response to a need. Typically, such a need will be rooted in powerlessness, poverty, or human indignity, three signs of the absence of the Kingdom of God. Each member of the group (however defined, by whatever affiliation) has a personal obligation to be just. Not only is it a personal obligation to be just in individual-to-individual and individual-to-group relationships, it is also a personal obligation to promote one's proper group response to social injustice.

So although I take the position that the just act of one person toward a disadvantaged person or group is not, strictly speaking, an act of social justice, I do not at all deny that an individual can place an act of social justice. Such actions would be taken within and toward one's own group in an effort to activate a justice response from that group toward another group. Perhaps I am being too restrictive. If so, it is only to make an important point about where education for social justice might best begin.

If education for social justice might be characterized as educating "men and women for others," it is important that attention be given to appropriate strategies and stages of the outward thrust. It will avail little if it is an isolated, individual initiative. This is not to say that isolated, individual initiatives are of no avail. Evidence to the contrary includes a glorious Christian tradition of heroic individual and even small-group initiatives. But despite these, the kingdom remains "at hand" as we move through the early years of the twenty-first century. It is still out of reach for the millions who experience powerlessness, poverty, and human indignity.

Education for social justice must begin with the group that impedes the flow of justice, that fends off a reign of justice and peace that has been "at hand" for nearly two thousand years. Such education must begin inside the Christian community, within its various groups and affiliations. Such education will have to be specialized as well as general. It will have to touch both young and old. It will have to be especially effective with those who have access to power. Education for social justice must be based on good theology and good social science. Social justice deserves a high place on the agenda of the intellectuals of the Church.

That which is to be understood and taught at all levels is a sense of solidarity with all of humankind, an awareness that solidarity means power, and an understanding of the techniques of organization needed to activate power. Whether power is directed toward just or unjust ends, as the Christian gospel defines them, depends in no small measure on whether or not the Christian conscience sets the direction of human activity. The challenge of all of this to Christian and Jesuit education is awesome; so too is the importance of the Christian educator. Let me conclude with a special word about the teacher in the task of social justice.

Sigmund Freud saw that a great person's influence on others would happen in two ways:

> . . . through his personality and through the idea for which he stands. This idea may lay stress on an old group of wishes in the masses, or point to a new aim for their wishes, or, again, lure the masses by other means.

Perhaps there is no older "group of wishes" in the people than the wish for justice, particularly that justice which the Christian tradition views as inextricably bound up with love. The Christian teacher who would educate for social justice must embody both love and justice at the level of personality and must internalize the justice-love integration as an "idea for which he stands." More is called for here than Greek impartiality or the "blind" justice of American jurisprudence. A bias toward the poor is called for. A sensitivity to powerlessness and indignity is essential for anyone hopeful of educating for social justice.

A sober self-assessment and practical humility should also accompany the teacher's approach to groups or individuals within groups. Such an assessment can be taken by reflecting on Henri de Lubac's words:

> If you are not yourself in a position to profit from injustice and if you do not have to make any effort to overcome this temptation, you must show complete moderation in your

manner of fighting injustice in others. It is important not to forget, too, that many who protest in the name of justice would only like—in good faith perhaps—to be the strongest and most favored themselves.

It is DeLubac who also offers the caution that "teachers of religion are always liable to transform Christianity into a religion of teachers." The Church is not a school; it is a community of believers, an incredible assembly of loved sinners. Such awareness is an indispensable part of the Christian perspective on education for social justice.

A teacher should be courageously prophetic. The truths about justice are not likely to comfort those who face a reduction in property, prestige, or power as the principles of justice gain wider acceptance. The prophetic teacher can expect resistance, rejection, and even unjust retaliation. But the quality of the great teacher, which is not always part of the prophetic charism, is the gift of patience. Some mistake this as timidity or unenlightened conservatism. But this need never be the case. What the teacher lacks in prophetic courage may be offset by a reserve of patience sufficient to retain serenity and peace of soul in an imperfect world where diverse peoples and nations are, by God's grace, becoming less and less unequal. The process is underway. The power to bring about a rule of justice resides in the Lord. The patient and persistent educator can help to lower the resistance and thus bring that hoped-for reign of justice that much closer in his or her own time.

As more teaching hands turn to the task of education for social justice, the rule of justice will remain less elusively "at hand" and become more fully grasped and comprehended. That's why Jesuit educational institutions can be good places to work for Jesuits interested in committing themselves to the service of faith and promotion of justice.

CHAPTER 5

The Enduring Evidence
of a Jesuit Education

There is a not-widely known Jesuit Association of Student Personnel Administrators (JASPA) that meets every five years on a Jesuit campus and convenes less formally at the annual meeting of the professional association that includes student-life administrators from across the board in higher education—institutions large and small, private and public, church-related and nondenominational. It is important for the Jesuit group to meet alone and apart from time to time because they know that they are different. They have a shared commitment and a common bond that relates to the Jesuit character of their schools. I've met with them several times; they helped me to shape the ideas I offer in this chapter.

Once when I was invited to share some thoughts with them, I attached this title to the presentation: "Seven Habits of Alumni We'd Be Proud to Call Our Own." Several years earlier, I had enjoyed reading Stephen R. Covey's longtime best-seller *The Seven Habits of Highly Effective People.*[1] That title kept circling in my mind as I thought about a workable structure for a conversation with student-life administrators from Jesuit institutions. The task I set for myself was to stimulate their thinking about the lifelong "proof" of the higher education "pudding" that is prepared in our Jesuit campus kitchens. Members of JASPA are not, I know, responsible for the entire pudding, but they have a critically important place in the total preparation of men and women for others, as we like to call our graduates. So I thought I'd like to invite them to think about the qualities they, and all of us who are involved in Jesuit education, would expect to find in alumni we would be proud to call our own.

I began by wondering whether I could identify seven or more habits of highly effective Jesuit college graduates. These alumni would be judged to be effective, I presumed, if they had something inside that was acquired during the collegiate experience and remained within to function as both compass and guide for principled, productive living in the postcollegiate years. There has to be more to it than pasting the higher education equivalent of an "Intel Inside" label on our graduates. Whatever the appropriate trademark might be, it will not be immediately noticeable. But those in careers for which they prepared in a Jesuit collegiate setting will, this theory goes, be in fact noticeably different.

In assembling this structure, sketching this outline, shaping this paradigm, I realized that I was proposing an ideal rather than documenting a verifiable experience. I have the imagination to do the former—propose the ideal—but lack the data to verify patterns of observable, after-graduation experiences of Jesuit alumni. Perhaps some institutions keep statistical tabs on their graduates and have interesting data. But most of us are not very good at outcomes measurement or, if we attempt it, do not track it consistently and coherently over the years. So we tend to discuss this at the level of theory rather than in terms of measurable results.

Habits, as philosophically aware Jesuit college graduates would know, are acquired by acting; you have to do—now and repeatedly—that which you want eventually to be able to do easily and habitually. The noun *habit* is derived from the Latin verb that means "to have." A habit is something you possess. Philosophically speaking, it is a quality, a principle of action, a modification of a substance. The seven habits I would expect to find driving the lives of Jesuit college alumni are habits (understood in the sense of principles of action) of

- reasoning
- reading
- writing
- reflecting
- praying
- helping
- giving thanks

Let me elaborate.

1. Reasoning

All successive stages of education depend on the basic skills of reading, writing, and reasoning. There is reasoning associated with the familiar third *R*—'rithmetic. This quantity-based, number-coded reasoning begins with arithmetic and gets abstract when the developing student meets algebra in middle or secondary school. Along the way, a habit of reasoning is taking shape, which, for most Jesuit college students, is shaped further by philosophy and other disciplines that are in the curriculum to encourage a well-rounded, "general" education. If it works the way it should, this kind of education produces a thinker, a person who can reason well, analyze clearly, and think things through along a logical path.

Now, as all student-life administrators know from observing the leisure habits of their charges, residence halls and student unions are typically not filled with avid, leisure-time readers. The image has more appeal than the printed word; high-volume sounds are more engaging than printed sentences. If anyone took the time to construct a financial ratio that would compare the dollar value of electronic audio and video hardware plus the matching software, CDs, DVDs, and downloads, on the one hand, against the value of the printed material in a typical resident student's room, on the other, the resulting ratio would, I suspect, be on the order of several hundred to one.

I don't think there is a whole lot that can be done to lower that ratio (which, by the way, will continue to grow with the multiplication of portable, out-of-the-room hardware like cell phones, iPods, and laptops), but creative extracurricular programming by campus professionals can do a lot to encourage better reasoning and productive reading in the out-of-class, out-of-library leisure hours of students. That leads me to the second habit I would hope to find well cultivated in the typical Jesuit college graduate—reading.

2. Reading

At the level of principle, the reading habit is driven by a conviction that the mind is a wonderful gift intended by God for our lifelong use. The lifelong quest for knowledge and truth is virtually impossible to pursue without reading good books. So a genuine Jesuit education will never, in my view, be achieved if reading stops when postcollegiate life begins.

Campus administrators can do a lot to promote authors—faculty authors by prominent display in the campus bookstore, other authors by invitation to campus for lectures and workshops. I've never seen it done, but I wonder why the student-affairs side of our shops could not initiate creative, high-profile cooperative programs with the campus library. There are, of course, outreach efforts from the libraries to help students gain familiarity with the new technologies. Our libraries now have their own addresses on the information highway and think of themselves as "learning resource centers." Student-personnel officers can do the students a great favor by using programming ingenuity and counseling opportunities to encourage their love of reading.

3. Writing

Similarly, the writing habit is evidence of a Jesuit collegiate experience that went according to plan. Several principles underlie the writing habit. One is the principle of self-realization: writing (not only creative writing) gives the writer a great sense of fulfillment. Another is the principle of participation: the writer interacts with the minds of his or her readers and participates in forming new ideas, changing cultures, and developing policies. And there is the principle of association with others in the cultivation and communication of ideas.

We are individuals in society. For personal development and societal enrichment, unique individuals must communicate. Moreover, this world of ours moves on words and numbers and communicates mainly by written and spoken words. Without mastery of both words and numbers, an individual will have little impact on the direction or pace of that movement and will thus make no significant contribution to human progress. Hence the Jesuit educational enterprise, dedicated as it is to human progress, will always emphasize communication and will systematically promote the ability to communicate in more than one language. The absence of communication skills is a sign of shortfall in Jesuit educational ideals. The absence of communication skills as a by-product of extracurricular activity on campus is a sign that the purely academic and the student-personnel sides of the house are not as closely linked as we would like to have them. On Jesuit campuses, at least, there is no argument about the desirability of connecting those two spheres of influence.

The well-reasoned argument (product of the well-trained mind) will find expression, according to the Jesuit educational expectation, in well-written and well-spoken form. A great deal is done on Jesuit campuses to promote writing skills by encouraging student publications. Student-affairs administrators sometimes regret that; they tend to get caught in the middle of publication-related controversies and freedom-of-expression issues. But they recognize that it would be good for students and universities if there were more encouragement and concern with creativity in these areas and less anxiety about censorship.

Habits of reasoning, reading, and writing are the infrastructure for principled behavior in four other areas of the postcollegiate life that we want our Jesuit alumni to enjoy: reflecting, praying, helping, and giving thanks.

4. Reflecting

Reflective persons are not impulsive; they are not necessarily indecisive (the opposite is almost always the case), but they are measured and deliberate in their approach to decision making. Reflection is the environment, the atmosphere, of ethical deliberation. And ethical reflection emerges from the "inner house," from the character of the one who deliberates and must decide. That character is shaped by the Jesuit educational experience. Not surprisingly, those who provide the educational experience—the Jesuits and their associates or partners in the enterprise—entertain the theoretical expectation of finding evidence of ethical decision making emerging over time from the characters of those in whose formation they have had a hand.

Whenever my thoughts turn to this issue, I find myself recalling the words of playwright Robert Bolt in the preface to his classic *A Man for All Seasons*. The play is a testimonial to the integrity and character of Thomas More. In the preface, written in 1960, Bolt explains his mood and his social perceptions as he wrote the play. He was troubled by the thin fabric of contemporary human character, by the tendency of the typical modern man and woman to think of himself or herself in the third person, to describe the self "in terms more appropriate to somebody seen through a window." Bolt then provides a penetrating insight amounting to a one-sentence summary of the cultural ills that beset us today: "Both socially and individually it is with us as it is with our cities—an accelerating flight to the periphery, leaving a center which is empty when the hours of business are over."[2]

The playwright goes on to ask, "Why do I take as my hero a man who brings about his own death because he can't put his hand on an old black book and tell an ordinary lie?" He answers:

> For this reason: A man takes an oath only when he wants to commit himself quite exceptionally to the statement, when he wants to make an identity between the truth of it and his own virtue; he offers himself as a guarantee. And it works. There is a special kind of shrug for a perjurer; we feel that the man has no self to commit, no guarantee to offer.[3]

Bolt describes Thomas More as "a man with an adamantine sense of his own self. He knew where he began and left off, what area of himself he could yield to the encroachments of his enemies, and what to the encroachments of those he loved." Jesuit higher education helps students gain a sense of self; they learn where they begin and where they leave off. We are concerned with filling up those empty centers when the hours of classroom and library business are over. We help students locate the presence or absence of principles in themselves. We encourage the cultivation of character, the exercise of principled judgment. We let our students know that we expect them to stand for something. This is not simply because we are faith-committed educators in Church-related institutions; it is because we think that standing for something is essential to experiencing full human life, to being human, to having character. Religious faith is, of course, important in our view, and it is religious faith that opens the door to the next habit in the set of seven that I put before the student-life administrators.

5. Praying

Prayer is part of the life of any believer; prayer is the periodic flame that rises from the continuous bed of embers we call faith. Reflection on faith and its implications for daily life is the work of theology, and theology is part of the Jesuit higher education experience. After graduation, theological reflection should continue. The relevance of religious faith to an earthbound career is a question that can be answered only by living one's faith in the world of work, family, citizenship, success, failure, illness, and death. The Jesuit collegiate experience—in class and in the broader campus context that includes liturgy and retreats—is designed to foster faith-based reflection for a lifetime.

Campus ministers normally enjoy a cooperative, even a collegial, relationship with student-personnel officials on Jesuit campuses. Those who minister pastorally to the faith needs of the campus community usually relate well to the academic side of Jesuit campuses. Many students will tell you of the impact a weekend retreat had on them during their undergraduate years. The senior retreat is often remembered as a positive rite of passage of far greater value than the commencement exercises.

Although interest of the young in formal religion may appear to be on the decline in many quarters, it is clear that an interest in spirituality is, for many, on the rise. I like to think of spirituality as prayer elevated to a lifestyle. It is not formal, devotional prayer; it is an awareness of the Spirit of God alive and active within my soul, wherever I—soul and body—may be. It is a sense of God present to me here and now, at my side, in these circumstances. Faith is the act by which I entrust myself to God; spirituality is the breathe-in, breathe-out environment in which that trust plays itself out in daily living.

No one, however, goes to God alone. Spirituality is not solipsism. Ignatian spirituality, the driving force behind retreat and ministry programs on Jesuit campuses, opens the eyes of the believer to the needs of others and thus impels the believer to become a man or woman for others.

It should be noted here that although not all beneficiaries of Jesuit education are Christian, the centrality of the person and gospel of Christ to the Jesuit spirit will be known to all and influential to many.

6. Helping

The habit of helping others—a habitual, principled openness to serving others in the human community—is expected of all Christians. Service, prompted by our love for one another, is a Christian characteristic; it is also a principle for action. The trademark is "This is how all will know that you are my disciples, if you have love for one another" (John 13:35). After washing the feet of his disciples on the night before he died, Jesus provided for all Christians a principle of action: "I have given you a model to follow, so that as I have done for you, you should also do" (John 13:15). If this ethic is not caught by participants in the Jesuit higher education process, that process has failed to deliver the product the enterprise is intended to produce.

This is why service learning is important in a Jesuit educational environment—important but, in my judgment, still generally underappreciated. Service learning is not just good pedagogy at work as, for instance, when lecture-hall instruction in a physical science is followed by laboratory opportunities for both application and assimilation of the principles. Those classrooms without laboratories—the ones used for theology and all the humanities—need community-service "labs" in settings of human need. There a student's hand, impelled by faith-based Christian love, extends the hand of Christ to reach a person in need of help. Again, it is the theoretical expectation of educators in the Jesuit and Catholic tradition that this faith-based, love-inspired readiness to serve will be evident in all stages of a graduate's life.

7. Giving Thanks

The habit of gratitude, of giving thanks, is a principle that must necessarily last a lifetime. Catholics, of course, find their identity in Eucharist (which means "thanksgiving"). As they meet in eucharistic assembly to remember the Lord in the breaking of the bread, Catholics are at once thanks-sayers, thanks-givers, and

thanks-doers. This deep, internalized sense of gratitude, this attitude of praise and thanks for the gift of redemption, is something
quite characteristically Jesuit; it should direct and sustain the
Jesuit educational enterprise.

Eucharist as sacramental food is nourishment for the faith journey. Eucharist as thanks is a habitual disposition that opens us up
in awe toward God and all the gifts of creation and then turns us
out of ourselves in a posture of generous service toward others in
the human community. And Eucharist as reconciliation gives us
all the more reason to be thankful because it has the power to heal
and forgive our failures to be of service, as we know we should, to
persons in need.

The internalization of this seventh habit, this principle of
behavior, is the work of classroom theology and campus ministry.
The practical application of the theory should be expected and
encouraged by student-personnel administrators throughout any
given student's undergraduate experience. Typically, this theory
should find expression in consideration for others on campus. We
know that there are many self-centered, even selfish, students on
Jesuit campuses; we have to help them overcome that selfishness.
Otherwise we fail them; we let them down.

Gross violations of consideration for others—in other words, serious violations of disciplinary codes—typically result in penalties
that go by the name *community service*. As a judicial sentencing category, *community service* is an unfortunate misnomer. Compensatory
service—making up or restoring to the community what was damaged or taken by an infraction of the rules—is what our disciplinary
codes should call for. Community service enacts an ethic that we
should expect to find in all our students as responsible members of
the campus community. It is a quality we would hope to find continuing on in the postgraduation lives of our alumni.

Show me a person who has cultivated the habits of reasoning
clearly, reading widely, communicating effectively, reflecting often,
praying faithfully, helping generously, and always giving thanks,

and I will show you evidence of a total Jesuit education. Any institution of Jesuit higher education hopes to have such persons show up for alumni reunions. And when they do, the system that produced them takes comfort in the realization that, indeed, there is nothing so practical as a great educational ideal.

Recently, I reread Robert K. Greenleaf's book *Servant Leadership.* He insists that any institution, for-profit as well as not-for-profit, must care about people. Leaders in industry, education, or any other type of organized activity are servants. This includes trustees—directors in Jesuit institutions as well as in for-profit corporate enterprises. "Clearly," says Greenleaf, "the trustees cannot take over and manage the universities. They have neither the time nor the competence to do this, and it is not their proper role. What then can they do? These things . . ."[4]

Here begins a list that I reproduce for the consideration of anyone interested in or responsible for governance on Jesuit campuses:

1. Insist that the goals of the university (and its major parts) be stated in clear, unequivocal, behavioral terms. What is supposed to happen? In what measurable ways should students be different after they have met the requirements?

2. Once the goals are stated, the trustees should then ask: "To what extent does the university now reach these goals, at a reasonable level of excellence, with the students it now has, and with resources it now has? If the discrepancy between the goals and the current state of the university is serious, the trustees should then ask for plans: "How can the gap be closed, and on what kind of timetable—in specific terms that can be measured and evaluated?"

3. If the internal constituencies cannot produce the plans or a reasonable timetable, the trustees may then suggest the engagement of consulting resources to help.

4. If, after a reasonable time, there is still a material gap between goals and performance and concrete plans for

better performance, the trustees might ask that the goals be scaled down to what is realistically achievable. If this is done, the trustees should ask that all the students be advised, as clearly and candidly as possible, just what help they can expect from the university. This is an age of great candor, and honesty has risen (commendably) as a student priority. The trustees should insist that this be respected.

5. As an alternative the trustees may have their own study made to try to find ways to set goals and propose innovations.

6. When the goals are realistically set and plans are fully made, the trustees should then attend to the top leadership of the university.

Anyone working in Jesuit education can substitute his or her job title for *trustee* in these Robert Greenleaf recommendations. And, of course, when it comes to attending "to the top leadership," all the rest of us should turn the searchlight on ourselves, not call for the replacement of higher-ups in the organization.

Assuming that you are now at work on a Jesuit campus, and assuming sufficient autonomy in managing your area of responsibility, you should begin to examine the goals of your division and be courageous enough to articulate clearly and in writing what you expect by way of behavior in the territory you govern and in the outcomes of the total educational process you are helping to provide for your students. This is a special application of the Ignatian examen. What do you stand for? If you come up empty in your response to that question, you will have ridiculously modest expectations of your graduates. If you really do stand for something Ignatian, something related to the formation of human character in those young men and women under your charge, you can look forward to the day when you will welcome returning alumni you will be proud to call your own. You will recognize them not as products but as persons of genuine quality, quality that lasts a lifetime.

CHAPTER 6

Discernment: A Spirituality of Choice

In Indonesia during the summer of 1995, I spoke to an international gathering of Jesuit business school deans and faculty on the topic "Education for Business in the Jesuit Tradition." This was a wonderful group of committed Jesuits and lay colleagues from all over the world; they met for several days at Sanata Dharma University, a Jesuit institution in the university city of Yogyakarta. Their focus was discovering the defining characteristics of Jesuit business schools, but they had a broader concern about building an international network for future faculty exchanges and program cooperation.

Unlikely as the prospect seemed when I first considered what I might say to this group, my presentation dealt with decision making in the Jesuit tradition. I thought there was much in the tradition that could be translated into decision-making processes in the schools themselves, as well as in the patterns of choice our students—most of them future managers—might follow. It proved to be a stimulating topic for discussion. There was widespread interest among lay colleagues in learning more about the tradition. The paper I gave on that occasion was translated into many languages for local consumption on the campuses from which these business educators came.

I began by pointing out that two questions found in the preface of a book published that year by the American Management

Association (AMA) had special relevance for the conversation we were opening up. These were good questions for anyone who is interested in fitting his or her spirituality (in our case, Ignatian spirituality) into workplace decision making. The book, *Transforming the Way We Work: The Power of the Collaborative Workplace* by Edward M. Marshall, was certainly not a spiritual tract, but here are the useful questions Marshall raises in his preface: "What would the world of work be like if we all truly respected one another? How effective would our workplaces be if we all knew how to collaborate?"[1]

Later in the book, the essence of Marshall's message is summarized:

> The new realities in business require a new type of leadership. Command-and-control no longer applies. Collaborative leadership, however, requires a significant shift in our relationships in the workplace. Since leadership is no longer a position but a function, and since everyone can be a leader, the responsibility for leading the organization shifts to the entire workforce. The traditional roles and responsibilities of leadership also change—from commanding to coaching, from telling to engaging, and from delegating to others to working with others. Our behaviors must change as we learn how to function in an environment of consensus formation, conflict resolution, and full responsibility.[2]

An Ignatian bell went off in my mind when I first read those words. I wanted to reflect on them and ponder their implications not only for how we act in the workplace but for how we prepare men and women for business in Jesuit schools.

In a Jesuit setting, faculty and students should be serious about exploring the relevance of religious faith to what happens in the workplace Monday through Friday, nine to five. The Jesuit setting fosters respect for anyone's honest faith commitment. It will come as no surprise to those who interact in Jesuit business schools that there is a connection, a genuine relevance, between anyone's religious faith and what happens on the job. There is, for example, a justice dimension to just about everything that happens at work. The prophet Micah said it well centuries ago: "You have been told, O man, what is good, / and what the Lord requires of you: / Only to do the right and to love goodness, / and to walk humbly with your God" (6:8). In other versions, those phrases are often translated "to act justly, to love tenderly, and to walk humbly with your God."[3] This is what spirituality can bring to the workplace, transforming it into a setting where those who come there to work are characteristically just and considerate in all they do.

Discernment of Spirits

I've been a member of the Jesuit order since 1950, as I indicated earlier. I learned early on that there is a theme in Jesuit spirituality that bears directly on the way you can search out God's will. It goes by the name of discernment—discernment of spirits. There is nothing secret or spooky about it; it is a centuries-old way of proceeding, a tested method of sorting things out so that you can make your way through the human predicament with some degree of confidence that you are following God's will in a particular set of circumstances. Discernment is a characteristically Jesuit way of testing the spirits, as found in the advice of 1 John 4:1: "Beloved, do not trust every spirit but test the spirits to see whether they belong to God, because many false prophets have gone out into the world." Or, to put "discernment of spirits" in the language of 1 John 4:6, "This is how we know the spirit of truth and the spirit of deceit."

Since discernment is part of me—part of my own personal spirituality—I was able to lay it out there in Indonesia and want to do that again here in these pages. As you consider the applicability of all this to your own life and to choices in the workplace, you will find yourself learning more about Jesuits than typically meets the most attentive eye!

I want to refer back to what I said in chapter 1 about Ignatius of Loyola, the founder of the Jesuit order, as we consider a little-known Jesuit way of coming to consensus—making choices, choosing a course of action—that has direct implications for building a collaborative workplace.

In his own words at the beginning of his *Autobiography* (written as a third-person narrative), Ignatius describes himself as a young adult: "Up to the age of twenty-six he was a man given over to the vanities of the world, and took special delight in the exercise of arms, with a great and vain desire for winning fame." An early biographer (Polanco, d. 1574) tells us that

> Iñigo's education was more in keeping with the spirit of the world than of God; for from his early years, without entering into other training in letters beyond that of reading and writing, he began to follow the court as a page; then he served as a gentleman of the Duke of Najera and as a soldier till the age of twenty-six when he made a change of life.[4]

This same biographer lists a few disciplinary lapses that would have had Iñigo tossed out of any modern Jesuit college or university:

> Up to the time [of his conversion], although very much attached to the faith, he did not live in keeping with his belief or guard himself from sins; he was particularly careless about gambling, affairs with women, brawls, and the use of arms; this, however, was through force of habit. But all this made it possible also to perceive many natural virtues in him.[5]

This last observation sounds like a later and typically Jesuit comment applied ironically, in this instance, to the youthful excesses of the man who would bring the Jesuit order into existence! A modern biographer notes, "As to what concerns the religious life of the Loyolas, we may say that it was, more or less, that of the people of Spain at that time. A profound and sincere faith and a substantial fidelity to religious practices was accompanied by moral lapses, which they themselves found no difficulty in admitting."[6]

Iñigo was seriously wounded by the French at Pamplona in May of 1521. A cannonball shattered his right leg and wounded his left. Immediate medical attention was ineffective, and he was sent home to the castle of his ancestors. The bones would not heal properly, so he chose (for reasons of vanity) to undergo another surgery.

During a long recuperation, Iñigo had his first reasoning, his first reflective experience, "of the things of God." It happened this way: The only books available in the house of Loyola to help him pass the time were a four-volume *Life of Christ* and another book containing selections from the lives of the saints. He read these, reflected at intervals as he worked his way through them, and noticed that his reflections were accompanied by feelings of warmth and attraction toward the person of Christ and the generous deeds of the saints. An alternative pastime was daydreaming, turning over in his imagination "what he would have to do in the service of a certain lady, the means he would have to take to enable him to go to the land where she was, the well-turned phrases and words which he would address to her, and the deeds of arms which he would do in her service."[7] This reflective imagining gave him an immediate feeling of pleasure that invariably dissolved into a feeling of dryness and discontent. He then found himself doing something of an "archaeology" on his contrasting moods, desires, and feelings. When he cut under them, he recognized that what was happening within him, in his "interior life," as the spiritual writers would put it, was a struggle between two competing forces, or spirits—one drawing him toward good, the other toward evil. His *Autobiography* mentions that "this was the first reflection he made on the things of God"; later on, when he was putting together his book of the Spiritual Exercises, it was "from this experience within him that he began to draw light on what pertained to the diversity of spirits."[8]

As Father Gerald Blaszczak, SJ, who was once responsible for introducing young Jesuits to Ignatian spirituality, put it, Ignatius began

> to conclude that the heart and its desires are the place where a woman or man with careful attention, with careful discrimination can find God's will revealed. That it is precisely in our hearts, with their panoply of desires, that we can discover a God who is anxious to reveal God's own heart, who is anxious to reveal God's own invitation to us. And so the rest of Ignatius's life is spent clarifying and watching his desires mature, and continuing to look for the desires which will galvanize his energies and center his efforts. . . . And he gathers people around him who are similarly captured by this desire. . . . And together, this desire to serve souls will lead them to do the most unexpected things, to go to the farthest corners of the world, and also to found schools, and colleges, and universities. . . . There is only one passion that centers their life, and it is simply to be of service.[9]

I recall once being of some assistance to a young woman who found herself at a career crossroads, an important decision point in her life. I encouraged her to focus on her feelings and deepest desires. I gave her an Ignatian idea from a non-Ignatian source, an ancient saying from the Upanishads. She carries it now, years later, tucked neatly in her address book: "You are what your deep driving desire is / As your desire is, so is your will / As your will is, so is your deed / As your deed is, so is your destiny."[10] Ignatius would remind us that love is shown in deeds, not words, and that our deeply felt desires are the place to begin looking for the direction in which God might be calling us to do great deeds.

A Method of Group Decision Making

Now I can begin to outline the method of group decision making, of choosing a course of action, that grew out of these Ignatian insights. It is traceable to the earliest deliberations of Ignatius and his first followers concerning the establishment of what is now known as the Jesuit order, and it is avowedly religious. Ignatius grew in his faith experience of God, as I mentioned, by taking an "archaeological" approach to his moods and feelings. He would also line his facts up before attempting a decision. Ignatian discernment includes judgment of fact and assessment of feeling.

Here's how it works: If a choice is to be made or an action taken, the relevant facts should be laid out first. This means having the necessary data and information in hand. On the basis of the available information, appropriate judgments of fact are made. Does this add up? Does it all compute? Do we have adequate and correct information?

After judgments of fact, the question is, What now shall we do? Options—each representing a plausible choice; each representing a relative good—are raised. Then the "goods" are weighed and measured against the feelings stirred in the decision maker in the face of any particular option.

Given a certain state of soul—for example, tranquillity or anxiety or dejection—Ignatius would have anyone interested in this method examine the origin of that feeling. Is the Spirit of God alerting me to something? Perhaps the origin of the mood is me; the feeling is no deeper than my selfish preference for the inertia of the status quo, and the anxiety is, in fact, resistance to change. Or perhaps an altogether different force can be operative—a diabolical influence referred to by Ignatius as the "evil spirit" and the "deadly enemy of our human nature." Ignatius had a tendency to see life as a struggle between the forces of good and the forces of evil. He saw God in all good things, but he was a realist who took careful account of the reality of evil in the world.

Ignatius had a healthy respect for what he saw as an adversarial relationship between divine and diabolical activity. In my opinion, contemporary believers who ignore this perduring reality do so at their peril. Christians are advised by the evangelist John: "Beloved, do not trust every spirit but test the spirits to see whether they belong to God" (1 John 4:1). Believers are also aware that the Spirit of Yahweh is active throughout biblical history. For instance, the Holy Spirit inspires (inspirits) the judges (Judges 3:10; 6:34; 11:29) and Saul (1 Samuel 11:6); the examples could be multiplied.

Acknowledging, then, the presence of divine activity in the world and a divine will for men and women and acknowledging the possibility of divine communication to humans (inspiration or "inspiriting"), believers, following the promptings not only of divine revelation but of logic and self-interest as well, consider it wise to count God in on their decision-making processes here and now. This calls for more than just a quick invocation or prayer of petition; the decision-making process has to be laced with a quest for God's will. Ignatius and his first followers did this relative to the structure, purpose, and organization of their company, the formal grouping of a committed band of brothers into what gained papal approval as the Company, or Society, of Jesus. What shape was this new enterprise to take? They processed the question in a structured, prayerful way and came up with an answer that produced not just acceptance but also peace in the hearts of all participants in the decision.

Based on that early experience, which is documented elsewhere,[11] the Jesuit procedure would have each participant in the group-decision-making process ask the following questions (note the relevance of group decision making to the collaborative workplace): How do I feel about the issue? What is the origin of that particular feeling? Is it from God, or not from God? The "not from God" feelings can be from self (from ignorance, obstinacy, indigestion), from other persons (whose position on this particular issue may be "not from God"), or from diabolical sources.

Prerequisites for a Good Discernment

To sort out all the elements, not only of the issue to be decided but also of the sources of my feelings related to that issue, is a subtle exercise. Even those who know the theory of spiritual discernment back away from the practice because of an unwillingness or inability to meet the four prerequisite demands. To discern or decide well, a person must be (1) ready to move in any direction that God wants, therefore radically free; (2) open to sharing all that God has given him or her, therefore radically generous; (3) willing to suffer if God's will requires it, therefore radically patient; (4) questing for union with God in prayer, therefore radically spiritual.

I realize that this discussion is moving into higher altitudes and thinner air than most of us are accustomed to, but there is clarity ahead, and even a few practical conclusions will soon be within reach. Jesuits would agree with former Speaker of the House Sam Rayburn's famous remark "When two people always agree about everything, it just goes to show that one of them is doing all the thinking!" We respect that. We also know that if union is to be achieved, it can only come out of difference. The point of the process I am outlining here is, in fact, to provide a method for moving from difference to consensus amicably and prayerfully. It is part of the Jesuit tradition. What a transformation (revolution?) that would mean for the typical workplace! And what a unique and attractive opportunity this way of proceeding offers to those who are willing to give it a try in the Jesuit workplace—in other words, school, college, university, parish, retreat house, research center, or any other collaborative setting.

It is true that group discernment grows out of personal holiness; it flowers in the communal process. It is not simply a matter of reflective common sense and informed prudence. Central to this method is the isolation of pros from cons, and the uninhibited expression of arguments, both pro and con, by each participant. Each is expected to disclose how he or she thinks (judges) the situation to be. An inclination "pro" will not hold up if it rests on inaccurate data. Is it true or false? is a question of intelligence or understanding.

Each participant is also to disclose how he or she feels about each side of the issue. Is it good or bad? is very much a question of feeling. And this is where discernment, the sorting out of feelings, comes in. This is what the early Jesuits did as they were deciding how best to design the very organization that would define them as Jesuits. Seeing something good on either side of a question is not insincerity or make-believe; any question important enough to become a policy issue certainly has two sides. But honesty requires that an effort be made to determine why each participant feels one way or another about a proposed option. "Disordered affections," as Ignatius would call them, can sabotage the work of intelligence and distort accurate judgments of fact.

Is there a place for conflict and positive persuasion anywhere in the process? Yes. But the appropriate place is in the initial phase of the process where the issue for discernment, the question to be decided, is formulated. Once the process is on the tracks, the discussion of positive and negative arguments should be separated. Contrary to what some might suspect, this saves time instead of wasting it. When debate (proper to the formulation stage) displaces dialogue (proper to the discernment process), ears and minds close, points are tallied, and a win-lose fulcrum falls into place, making the process vulnerable to the loudest voice, the greatest threat, or the highest emotion. Repair meetings are needed, which often fail to prevent unwise decisions. The Jesuit method is totally civilized, basically religious, and properly nonviolent. What's more, it works!

How does the group know it has reached a good decision? What confirmation does it have that the divine will has been perceived and followed in this particular case? The Jesuit tradition puts the premium on peace as the confirmatory factor. Each person should ask, "Am I at peace with this decision? Am I at ease now, especially if what I antecedently regarded as the best course of action is not the one chosen by the group consensus? Or am I uneasy?"

It is my personal view that a group is well on its way to good decision making if everyone in the group feels free to express, in the presence of the others, any unease he or she may feel about the issue before them, which is much easier if subjective reactive feelings have been shared very early in the process. After the decision is made, the disappearance of that unease is, I think, sufficient confirmation that God's will is working in the group. No vote was taken. No disgruntled minority remains. Group unity is substantially enhanced.

Another useful norm is the consistency or inconsistency of the decision with the statement of purpose that constitutes the corporate vision of the group (a mission or goal statement). If the decision is consistent with the shared vision, you have another confirmatory factor in place. Let me just note the obvious mischief waiting to break out if any participant in the process does not really share—in the sense of buying into—the vision of the group. Anyone who remains uncommitted to the vision (the declared purpose or mission) of the organization or group has no rightful place in deciding the future of that organization or group.

What is the relevance of all this to laypeople in business or other areas of the world of work? What is the relevance of this to laypeople who work with Jesuits? This is another way of asking what the relevance of religious faith is to business or professional practice. If this kind of decision making has no relevance in the workplace, then what, if anything, of what we do on Sunday can spill over into our Monday-through-Friday responsibilities? And it goes without saying that there should be room for this kind of group decision making in the Jesuit workplace.

Recall that the workplace setting is changing. Social and economic forces are "transforming the way we work," as the AMA book title cited at the opening of this chapter puts it. A new respect is emerging for "the power of the collaborative workplace," as that same publication's subtitle suggests. Who can say that spiritual forces are not also at play, along with the social and economic, to prompt these workplace developments? I would never concede that there is no place for faith-based decision making in corporate America today. Indeed, more of this sort of thing may be precisely what corporate America needs. To the extent that Jesuits and their lay collaborators apply this decision-making approach in their schools, the probabilities increase of seeing the method spill over into secular decision-making circles.

Men and women of faith cannot remain faithful while ignoring the invariant God when they shrewdly examine "all the variables" in a decision-making process. But how, you ask, can they do this without looking silly, wasting time, or converting the enterprise into a monastery? Here are a few suggestions that I made at the gathering of Jesuit business educators in Indonesia; they are applicable, I pointed out, to what we teach our students to do as future managers and to how we conduct our business on Jesuit campuses.

Bringing Discernment Down to Earth

Look at your charter, mission statement, papers of incorporation, brand name, motto, or slogan. Is there room for the admission that your organization, like your nation, operates "under God"? If so, reaffirm that fact and determine not to hide it at the policy-making table. If not, then at least acknowledge the power and presence of the group as larger than the power and presence of any one participant (including the boss!) and expect more from the group than could come from the individual.

Have a little quiet time before and during decision-making meetings. In many cases it would be a good idea for top management or group leaders to take a few days off for a communications workshop or a management retreat to dissolve interpersonal tensions, reduce anxiety levels, and open members of the decision-making group to the possibility of exchange of feelings and subjective views. Mutual trust is a sine qua non for good group decisions.

Allow for full participation in the preparation of the agenda, with provision for strong advocacy of a position early in the meeting process. Make careful provision for the accumulation and assimilation of all necessary information.

Provide opportunities for all elements of unease to surface, followed by a quiet time when each participant can reflect on the possible sources of his or her own unease.

Segment the meeting into time "pro" and time "con" with respect to every major issue. In each of these segments, all participants must speak, if only to agree with a point already made.

Whoever chairs the process then tries to "read a consensus" and tests it against the group. If there is no clear consensus, the chair can probe for areas of consensus. At this juncture, some open debate may be useful. As a last resort, the group can decide by vote.

Confirmatory procedures will evolve as the group gains experience with the process.

This method is well suited to what psychologist Kenneth Keniston and others began in the 1960s to call "the postmodern style." Keniston says, "A focus on process rather than on program is perhaps the prime characteristic of the postmodern style, reflecting a world where flux and change are more apparent than direction, purpose, or future."[12] Men and women in business tend to drive directly toward program decisions as the target or output of group meetings. Too little attention is paid to process on the way to program or even to process as an end, or program, in itself. As a consequence, valuable human interaction is plowed under by neatly cut programs to which the group is unevenly committed. The prognosis for subsequent success in executing such programs is not good.

The output of a good discernment process is *clarity*. The direction of an ongoing decision-making group is from clarity to clarity. In this sense, planning is iterative and unmistakably human, not inhumanly mechanical. What I attempted to do in Indonesia and want to repeat here is to emphasize that awareness of divine activity in the midst of a group serves to enhance both the *humanity* (the process begins with the feelings) and the *quality* of a group's decisions. By making a little room for God in their daily lives, organizational men and women will maximize their enlightened and clarified self-interest. Their actions will demonstrate that the word of the Lord, as received from Isaiah, is to be taken seriously: "I was ready to be approached by those who did not consult me, ready to be found by those who did not seek me. I said, 'I am here, I am here,' to a nation that did not invoke my name. Each day I stretched out my hand to a rebellious people who went by evil ways, following their own whims, a people who provoked me to my face incessantly" (65:1–3, JB).

The Jesuit is convinced that inner peace can be found through the discernment process, which leads to decisions that embody clarity. Full respect must be given, however, to the preconditions: freedom, generosity, patience, and a desire to find union with God in prayer. No believer should ever forget that the outstretched hand of God is always there to help.

Even if an individual or group falls short in meeting the preconditions, much can be learned from attempting and participating in the process. It will reveal how leadership as "function" can replace leadership as "command-and-control position," once the latter is seen by all to be anachronistic (and that day is probably already here!).

A Spirituality of Choice

In the spirit of full disclosure and truth in advertising, let me end this chapter on a qualifying note. What I have described here as a Jesuit approach to decision making is authentically and historically Jesuit. It is not, however, ordinary practice among contemporary Jesuits faced with the challenge of group decision making. Some Jesuit communities attempt it (we did it successfully at Georgetown in 1997 in deciding about future living arrangements), but the practice is not widespread or common. Like any other human group, Jesuits—companions who are members of the Company—do not find it easy to rein in individualistic tendencies and self-interest. Nonetheless, many individual Jesuits do in fact practice this kind of discernment, beginning with an examination of their feelings, in their own personal approach to decision making. Jesuit spirituality is a spirituality of choice.

What Jesuits do privately and personally along these lines influences their way of moving toward consensus in their dealings with colleagues, lay and Jesuit, in the workplace. What non-Jesuits may have gained from this overview of the inner workings of Jesuit spirituality may be helpful not only in their continuing personal search for God's will but also in their collaborative decision making with Jesuits. Against this background, all of us who live the Ignatian spirit and work in the Jesuit tradition should be more inclined to pay attention to our feelings as we face decisions, large or small, in our lives. The head, however, remains very much a part of the process. As Patrick Heelan, the Jesuit philosopher of science, remarked one time to me, Ignatian discernment "helps you find your place in the world and read it correctly."

Before any major decision is made, the decider, in the Jesuit tradition, will want to ask how he or she feels when considering the options. Once sources of the feeling are identified and clarified, the decider will be better able to choose and, in making the decision, more likely to find his or her will aligned with the will of God. Even if alignment with God's will is not a major concern for you in approaching a decision that will affect you in the workplace, tuning in to your feelings before you decide is still a good idea.

The Washington-based executive search consultant Jonathan E. McBride says in a "Manager's Journal" essay for the *Wall Street Journal* that when he is asked to counsel a promising candidate for a position, he often finds himself saying, "If your head says 'go' and your heart says 'no'—don't do it; if your heart says 'go' and your head says 'no'—give it a whirl. You can usually find facts to support your feelings; you can't really massage your feelings around to support the facts."[13]

When I asked Jon McBride about the relevance of all that I've laid out in this chapter to a specific decision of taking or not taking a particular job opportunity, he said that it is always wise to start with the feelings. "Career decisions will be more successful and more rewarding," he told me, "when the candidate's head and heart both embrace a job-changing decision." I would add this characteristically Jesuit perspective to that comment: the believer can count on finding God there at the intersection of head and heart.

A brochure that describes the Center for Ignatian Spirituality at Boston College offers a clear and concise response to the question, What is Ignatian spirituality? I use the following paragraphs to summarize the spirit that we Jesuits want to share with our lay colleagues, students, alumni, and friends:

> Ignatian spirituality originates out of the experience of Ignatius Loyola (1491–1556), a Basque courtier, who during a period of enforced convalescence from battle wounds, gradually awakened to the action of God in his life. Then, through a prolonged period of introspective struggle, this self-designated "pilgrim" came to an experiential understanding of how God works within the human heart. In works like the *Spiritual Exercises*, the *Autobiography*, the *Constitutions of the Society of Jesus*, and his correspondence with his companions, Ignatius has left a rich store of spiritual wisdom. This wisdom centers on the conviction that God deals directly with any man or woman who seriously seeks for meaning and direction in life and that God can be found anywhere.
>
> For Ignatius God's action leads to peace and commitment, peace with oneself and commitment to help others. Consequently, Ignatius emphasizes magnanimity, a generous willingness to work for great enterprises, especially those that help the greatest number of people and have the most enduring results. For Ignatius the prime example of a life lived generously for a great enterprise is Jesus Christ; and that conviction explains, in large part, his insistence that the order he founded be called the Company or Society of Jesus.

Throughout his spiritual teaching, Ignatius stresses the principle of adaptation. By that he means that God works with respect for the freedom of each individual, with regard for the history, temperament, and talents of each man or woman. Ignatian spirituality, then, is about encounter not performance, about freedom not manipulation, about individual choice not group pressure. Consequently, Ignatian spirituality invites ecumenical participation, inculturation, and interreligious dialogue.

CHAPTER 7

Living Generously in the Service of Others

When graduates of Jesuit schools, colleges, and universities from around the world came together for several days in Sydney, Australia, not long ago, I was invited to keynote the meeting by spelling out, in any way I liked, the theme: What values should Jesuit alumni and other people of faith bring to the twenty-first century?

I began that keynote address with reference to a research project I conducted that involved interviews with 150 American men and women, ages forty to fifty-five, who had lost their white-collar managerial jobs and were in an involuntary state of career transition. They were out of work and on the street, victims of what business writers came to call "downsizing." The American economy was at that time, according to the London *Economist*, in a condition of "corporate anorexia."

Interviews with Jesuit Alumni

I wanted to learn from these displaced managers how they coped with what for most was a personal, family, and career crisis; I wanted to discover what sustained them as they traveled the uncertain road to reemployment. I especially wanted to identify the principles that drove them and their job-search strategies. This research project put me in touch with several interesting Jesuit alumni. One of them told me that in an effort to boost his spirits in this very dark period of his life, he found himself falling back on lessons learned in humanities courses three decades earlier at Marquette University in Milwaukee, Wisconsin.

During his search for work, said this financial-services executive, "I kept coming back to my college English courses and a line from G. K. Chesterton's 'The Ballad of the White Horse.'" He remembered that line as "They harden their hearts with hope." The line, as Chesterton wrote it, reads, "And Alfred, hiding in deep grass, / Hardened his heart with hope."[1] The man I interviewed explained that he understood these words to mean, "Don't tell me it's not going to work. I can do it." Elsewhere, in his famous 1905 book *Heretics*, Chesterton wrote, "It is only when everything is hopeless that hope begins to be a strength at all. Like all Christian virtues, it is as unreasonable as it is indispensable."[2]

This Marquette alumnus personally had to rely on that kind of hope twice in situations of job loss, he told me, and he often used Chesterton's expression to encourage others in similar circumstances. Another line from "The Ballad of the White Horse" refers, as he recalled it, to "the giant laughter of Christian men."[3] "Here were men," this job seeker mused, "ostensibly on the verge of being exterminated, and they were laughing!" He derived from this literary snippet a guiding principle for dealing with adversity. He stated it simply: "You can't afford to lose your sense of humor."

As men and women who bear the stamp of a Jesuit education, what values might you be expected to carry with you, I asked the Sydney delegates, as you prepare to move into the twenty-first century? Would hope and humor be among them, I asked, as they were and continue to be for the Marquette alumnus just described?

I then told the story of another Marquette alumnus whom I interviewed in the course of my study.[4] This fifty-one-year-old man was president and chief operating officer of a small graphics company in the Chicago suburbs. He reported directly to a working chairman. Just before he was ready to leave home for work one morning, his wife passed along some bad news she had received the day before: she had breast cancer. Her husband was stunned, saddened, and understandably upset. He wanted to stay with his wife that day, but it was simply impossible. An important meeting was scheduled with people coming in from out of town; he absolutely had to attend.

When he arrived at work, his chairman saw that something was wrong. "John," he said, "you look upset. What's the problem?"

"I just got some bad news," John replied. "Pat has breast cancer."

"Well, John," the chairman responded, "maybe you ought to get all your bad news on the same day. I'm afraid I've got to let you go."

John was reeling—for the second time within only a few hours. Although he had received a handsome pay raise just weeks before, he decided not to fight the dismissal. He later told me that he realized he had been trapped for some time in a dysfunctional situation. Best to break away promptly, he thought, and get home to take care of his wife. As if he needed further proof that he was working for the wrong organization, John soon discovered that his contractually assured twelve-month severance period had been unilaterally cut to six, and the 100 percent compensation that was to continue for a year in the event of involuntary separation had been cut in half.

After reviewing all the options, John decided not to litigate, choosing instead to get on with his life and help his wife get on with hers. (Both, by the way, are now doing fine. John is running his own company, and Pat is in remission.) "We were the best of friends when we got married," John later told me in Pat's presence, "and having been through all this together, we're better friends today." These two met at Marquette, where they began to incorporate into their lives the values they were invited to consider during their student days—commitment, integrity, caring concern, faith, hope, and love. These, John told me, are the values he subsequently used to build a successful business of his own.

These anecdotes from the lives of Jesuit alumni enabled me to put the keynote question another way and personalize it to this audience: What might the great educational tradition that helped shape your minds and hearts during your student years expect you to contribute—through your minds and hearts, your very lives—to the culture of the new millennium, to your family culture, your business culture, your national or professional culture? What will you bring to any sphere of influence that might be yours?

A Distinctive Culture

A culture, in the words of the late and great Canadian Jesuit theologian Bernard Lonergan, "is a set of meanings and values informing a common way of life, and there are as many cultures as there are distinct sets of meanings and values."[5] What, therefore, are the meanings and values that make a community of Jesuit alumni? What is it that Jesuit alumni hold in common? What is distinctive about the shared meanings and values that are characteristic of them? And how might the culture that is the expression of the Jesuit heritage not simply defend but also gain ground against the competing, and even contradictory, sets of meanings and values that are present now or likely to emerge in the next millennium?

What is distinctive about the shared meanings and values that Jesuit alumni hold? I acknowledged that this question may not have received much thought in the past. Perhaps this audience, given its cultural diversity, would not come to immediate agreement there and then on a precise answer to that question. Perhaps they would find it difficult or impossible, even after careful reflection and with the best of intentions, to reach consensus on this point. Meanings of great significance to some may be of little importance to others. Values firmly held by some may be disvalues in the eyes of others.

I recalled a discussion paper drafted by a group of faculty and administrators at Georgetown that was developed in connection with a strategic plan for the entire university. This document

reaffirmed "the Jesuit conception of education as pursuit of knowledge in service of the world." It spelled out this notion in the following words, which I still find compelling:

> Georgetown seeks to be a place where understanding is
> joined to commitment; where the search for truth is informed
> by a sense of responsibility for the life of society; where aca-
> demic excellence in teaching and research is joined with
> the cultivation of virtue; and where a community is formed
> which sustains men and women in their education and their
> conviction that life is only lived well when it is lived gener-
> ously in the service of others.

Notice the four themes:

Commitment

Responsibility (for the life of society)

Cultivation of virtue

Conviction that life is only lived well when it is lived generously in the service of others

Reduce these four themes to four words: commitment, responsibility, virtue, and service.

Jesuit alumni may find themselves divided in their understandings of what commitment, responsibility, and virtue entail. And
although a common understanding of service might be easily
reached, a commitment to the proposition that "life is only lived
well when it is lived generously in the service of others" may not be
shared. That would, in my view, be regrettable, but it is quite possible in any disparate group of graduates of Jesuit schools.

There will be hesitancies and contingencies, I suspect, surrounding any effort to identify a set of meanings and values shared
by Jesuit alumni worldwide. But this is not to say that the effort
should not be made. I proceeded to make that effort by directing
the attention of the audience to the words of two Basques. They

lived centuries apart. Their faith-based convictions established (in the case of one) and profoundly influenced (in the case of the other) the Jesuit heritage. Ignatius of Loyola, born in 1491, founded the Jesuit order in 1540. Pedro Arrupe, born in 1907, served as superior general of the Jesuit order from 1965 to 1983.

As I indicated earlier in these pages, *to help souls* is the expression found most frequently in the writings of Ignatius when he wanted to describe the purpose of the company he established—the movement we now know as the Society of Jesus. *Helping others* is the phrase contemporary Jesuits use to explain whatever it is they are doing in a variety of ministries in all corners of the world.

The most remembered words of Pedro Arrupe will, I believe, prove to be those he spoke to the Tenth International Congress of Jesuit Alumni of Europe in Valencia, Spain, on July 31, 1973. After noting that "education for justice has become in recent years one of the chief concerns of the Church," he said:

> Today our prime educational objective must be to form men-for-others; men who will live not for themselves but for God and his Christ—for the God-man who lived and died for all the world; men who cannot even conceive of love of God which does not include love for the least of their neighbors; men completely convinced that love of God which does not issue in justice for men is a farce.

The entire address was controversial because it called for change and pointed the Society of Jesus clearly in the direction of the promotion of social justice. The men-for-others theme (later edited to read "men and women for others") soon spread all over the world and gained ever wider acceptance in Jesuit educational circles.

Both themes—helping others and becoming men and women for others—are today not simply descriptive but also definitive of Jesuit life and work. They are intended to be a formative influence in the minds and hearts of those who are touched by Jesuits, Jesuit ministries, and Jesuit institutions. And all three—Jesuits, Jesuit ministries, and Jesuit institutions—are expected today to be faithful extensions of their Jesuit heritage by focusing on service and working for faith-based justice.

I used to ask friends to exercise their imaginations and look into the faces of my students in my Georgetown course "Social Responsibilities of Business." The students were all seniors, more than half were female, and about one-third were foreign born. If you were to look through their faces, so to speak, and run a straight-line projection out thirty or forty years, you would be looking at women in high levels of executive responsibility, and you would see both men and women of cultural sensitivity feeling quite at home in a global marketplace. Many of these young men and women—now well established as Jesuit alumni—are and will continue to be men and women of faith. It is interesting to speculate on the degree to which they will remain or become men and women for others. I used to ask them all at semester's end to compose a personal mission statement that would set the direction for their future lives. Here are excerpts from the statements of three young women whom I had in class. The first wrote:

> To live out my belief that God's presence on Earth is manifested in others and in myself. This belief imparts to me a responsibility to treat others with the utmost respect and dignity as one would treat God, and to behave as God would—to exhibit love, energy, and the wisdom of experience at all times.
>
> I am committed to service to the communities in which I reside and in which I will reside. I am alert to opportunities to participate in the life of my communities. I am especially dedicated to the service of women, children, schools, and the natural environment.

The second student wrote:

> I am a twenty-one-year-old woman who is half Chinese and half Greek, and who grew up in Kuwait. I feel Greek, but I'm not sure what it is that makes the Greek side of

my heritage so dominant. I am very interested in advertising and I would like to work in the account management department of a large advertising firm in London or New York. I want to give back to the community in any way I can. I believe that in the advertising industry there is a lot of room for socially responsible behavior. I plan to have a positive effect on society through the products I will promote and the methods I will use to promote them. I will be a wife and mother. My children will come before my work and before my personal life. Through my children, I will give back to society.

And the third student put her personal mission statement in these words:

I've spent most of my life thus far studying, and during the most recent years pursuing two particular paths of interest: international business and the Russian language and culture. For as long as I can remember, I have been drawn to and fascinated by Russia—its people, history, language, and culture. This is actually why I began to study business. I think that business is potentially a great means by which one can help people, by providing new products and improving their living standard. It is my goal to create some sort of mutually beneficial relationship, wherein there is a sharing of resources and a fulfilling of needs. I know that although it may not be possible for one person to help the world, it is possible for one to help a few.

During the course of my life I intend on extending my family. I think that children are miraculous creations; and although I don't know at what stage of my life or how many I want to have, I cannot wait until the day when I will be a mother. Although I have my fears, just like everyone else, I hope that I will never be afraid to reach out to others, and to give them everything I can.

These are just samplings of the responses my students made to an assignment to write a mission statement that would have no impact at all on their course grade but would, if they chose to let it happen, serve as a guide and checkpoint for their progress through life. It was striking to me that issues relating to the heart of the Jesuit heritage were alive in the minds and hearts of these young women while still students at Georgetown.

The question is always open as to whether Jesuit alumni are ready to permit themselves, as men and women who bear the stamp of a Jesuit education, to be *described* as truly concerned with helping others and *defined* as men and women for others. If not all, most? If not most, then what might be done to plant this heritage in the minds and hearts of those who remain untouched by these themes? As the few examples of student thought that I just presented attest, there is encouragement to be drawn from listening to our youngest alumni.

Not all Jesuit alumni are Catholic; not all are Christian. There are Jews, Hindus, Muslims, and Buddhists on our alumni rolls, as well as men and women of relatively unknown faiths or no faith at all. They have, however, at least two things in common: possession of the same human nature, and the experience of a Jesuit education intended to nurture and release their unique human potential.

As I indicated earlier, the explicit expectation of Jesuit education today is to nurture in its students a commitment to be men and women *for others*. This is a value commitment, a commitment to work for justice and peace, a commitment (for those who profess the Christian faith) to the service of faith through the pursuit of justice. And implied in all of this is a requirement on the part of each to respect the faith commitments of all.

Four Enduring Characteristics

Reflect with me now on commitment, responsibility, virtue, and service. And ask, as you reflect, whether and why Jesuit education is truly the "pursuit of knowledge in service of the world."

Commitment. Although we normally think immediately of commitment *to* a person or cause, it is wise to pause and think of what, if anything, we have to commit. What we have to commit, of course, is the self. You have a self, your own self, to commit. The person with no real self to commit is a person of no character, a person of no depth. Jesuit education focuses on the care of the person and the cultivation of his or her personal human potential. Jesuit alumni are persons who are taking a voyage of self-discovery. They have a place to stand. They have a sense of place in the human community and the world of ideas. They hold common ground from which they can exercise their conviction that "life is only lived well when it is lived generously in the service of others."

Contemporary secular cultures, dominated by values that are alien to the culture of a Jesuit campus, are inhospitable to the notion of permanent commitments. We notice this in the way the young approach career and marriage commitments. Secular cultures are littered with broken promises. They encourage the postponement of commitment; in a complete misunderstanding of freedom, they celebrate the uncommitted life. In an age like ours where goals are ambiguous, there will inevitably be an emphasis on process over product, on endless undirected process in an unguided search for ever-elusive meaning.

Responsibility. Responsibility is the second keystone value. It is responsibility "for the life of society" that the Georgetown statement emphasized. Those who have a place to stand, who—as Robert Bolt wrote of Thomas More—know where they begin and where they leave off, have a responsibility to help society by doing what they can to halt the drift, to offer direction and guidance through the participation of their committed selves in the flow of history.

"Some are guilty; all are responsible" was the wise remark of Rabbi Abraham Joshua Heschel in considering injustices and destruction in the world around him in the 1960s. Blame is no substitute for analysis (which comes naturally to Jesuit alumni), but analysis will become paralysis unless responsibility translates itself into the effective action of responsiveness. Jesuit spirituality is a spirituality of choice. The Jesuit heritage offers centuries of evidence of informed action following deliberate choice. And all action, in the Jesuit tradition, is for the greater glory of God.

God, in the Jesuit view, is to be found and served in the work of building not a Tower of Babel but a new Jerusalem, a better society. And this construction project is undertaken by exercising responsibility for the life of society.

Virtue. The word *virtue* means "strength." Who among us is strong enough to meet the challenges of life unassisted? And what assistance can substitute for the help of God?

Jesuit education is education of the heart, cultivation of the will, development of the mind; it is a celebration of the person— body and soul, mind and heart—striving for excellence.

The virtues are essential ingredients of a Jesuit education. Faith, hope, and love are called theological virtues because their ultimate object is God. All three of these virtues are part of a Jesuit education, which, as every scribbling schoolboy jotting "AMDG" on the top of an assignment sheet knows, is provided *ad majorem Dei gloriam.* Nor will any Jesuit alumnus fail to recognize traces of the so-called cardinal virtues in his or her educational experience; prudence, justice, temperance, and fortitude were laced through the lessons, highlighted in the literature, and embodied in the lives and good example of the teachers, the dedicated providers of Jesuit education.

The moral theologian James F. Keenan, SJ, has proposed his own list of the cardinal virtues: justice, fidelity, self-care, and pru-dence.[6] The point of substituting fidelity and self-care for the tra-ditional temperance and fortitude is not to suggest that there is nothing left to fear nor any threat of excess in modern life; it is simply one expert's effort to make our understanding of right liv-ing become more effectively transcultural and transgenerational. This is helpful if for no other reason than to make the point that a worldview characteristic of Jesuit alumni should be comfortable with what I like to call the distinction between the shrub and the seed, or the tree and the acorn.

My Australian Jesuit friend Peter Steele explained to me how early-nineteenth-century landscape painters working in one country (British painters, for example, working in Australia) tended to depict the foreign country's trees in shapes and colors proper to the painter's native land—clear evidence of monoculturalism or cultural isolation, if not insensitivity.

Evangelists who, figuratively speaking, uproot the church as they know it ceremonially, linguistically, and ritually in their home country and set out to transplant that tree in foreign soil also demonstrate a great cultural insensitivity. Their efforts are going to bring them into conflict with the culture they hope to evangelize. It would be a wiser and far more effective strategy for them to think of the good news of salvation not as a tree but as seed to be planted in other fields where soil conditions and local rains, winds, climate, minerals, and light will give a special size and shape to that which grows from the seed. The same seed would grow into different shapes and sizes if planted elsewhere.

Keenan's "virtue ethics" would leave it to each culture to "fill each virtue with its specific material content and apply it practically" to local conditions. Accordingly, Jesuit alumni would be men and women of virtue even though culturally diverse. Their virtues would, in Keenan's words, be "about right actions coming from rightly ordered and virtuous persons."

Service. Our fourth keystone is service, which for Jesuit alumni might be thought of as both action (turning talent inside out) and attitude (facing outwards). Recall that we are considering "the Jesuit conception of education as pursuit of knowledge in service of the world." Once that knowledge is acquired, the pursuit turns to service, to searching out and meeting human need.

An old African proverb advises, "God gives nothing to those who keep their arms crossed." So we should open up our arms to others, reach out to others with a helping hand. Jesuit alumni who are educated to become men and women for others are men and women of open arms.

Privatizing Tendencies

With the rise of affluence in parts of the world where most, but by no means all, Jesuit alumni live, there has been a proliferation of socially atomizing appliances. We think it not at all unusual to have a private car, a single-family home, a personal phone (on your desk, in your car, and in your pocket), a stationary or portable fax, computer, radio, television set, and iPod. Most of us have ready access to a freezer, a microwave oven, and a host of other appliances. An automatic washer and dryer are ready and nearby. We rarely have to ask anyone for anything to meet our daily needs. Without a conscious choice on anyone's part, we are now, for all practical purposes, sealed off from the human interaction previous generations enjoyed at the village well, the general store, the daily food market, the bus or train depot, and the public gathering places for recreation, worship, and communication. Not so very long ago, these points of contact were routine—even indispensable—parts of ordinary life. Now, in their absence or diminished presence, a commercially sanctioned culture of loneliness, isolation, and alienation has set in.

You have to deal with this first in yourself, and the best way to do that is through service to others. You have daily opportunities to assist neighbors and others as they make their way through their similarly privatized, atomized lives.

Tom Mahon, a technology-marketing consultant in the San Francisco Bay Area, writes, "Science and technology deal with things: atoms and galaxies, levers and microprocessors. The life of the spirit, on the other hand, deals with the connections between things: mercy, justice, and love. We have become very good in the age of science and technology at knowing about things, but we're not really as wise as we should be at making connections."[7]

A Jesuit education prepares you to raise your head above the short-term chaos to notice that there are connections waiting to be made. You can make them. Helping others is the way to make those connections real. Never forget that helping others and becoming men and women for others are the characteristics that define the common ground on which Jesuit alumni worldwide are proud to stand.

I recall having lunch with a Jesuit alumnus who is a well-known and influential journalist in Washington. I asked him what he values from the eight years of Jesuit education that had ended for him about thirty-five years earlier. He replied that he had something that graduates of other very good schools did not possess. "You taught us to take a set of facts, connect those facts, and draw right conclusions," he said. "You taught us how to think, how to reason through the facts." That response would match up with the post-graduation experience of many Jesuit alumni.

Some would have other ways of describing what they have carried with them over the years from their exposure to Jesuit education. One put it this way for me: "You showed us where north is." Another recalled his Jesuit schooling as the experience of "something that came as close to being a pure meritocracy as I have ever known." He had neither money nor social standing, he said, yet in his high school days he came together with others in a single place where he was "educated and treated equally." He added, "It all had the effect of generating a wonderful esprit de corps."

Forging connections and using reason would figure often in alumni responses to the question of what they gained from their Jesuit education. In the replies of younger alumni, phrases like *commitment, responsibility for the life of society, the cultivation of virtue* (especially justice), and *the conviction that life is lived well only when it is lived generously in the service of others* are now occurring with more frequency and are likely to be heard more often as the great tradition of Jesuit education moves forward into the unknown future.

CHAPTER 8

The Celibate: A Crowd of One

One of the puzzling aspects of Jesuit life—for those who observe it or consider it as a vocational choice, as well as for those who live the Jesuit vocation—is the question of celibacy. It is more than a puzzle; it is a mystery.

Many Jesuits spend large segments of their lives doing exactly what many lay colleagues do with their professional lives—teaching, lecturing, researching, writing books and articles, administering complex organizations. The Jesuit academic asks himself from time to time, "Why do I give up marriage when I could have a wife and family and still do what I do as an academic professional (although I could not, of course, do with my remaining time what I now do on the side, so to speak, as a priest-pastor)?" Celibacy is part of the answer to that question—celibacy not as baggage to be lugged along on life's journey but as an apostolic reality linking the celibate to the saving mission of Jesus. Moreover, celibacy is what theologians call "an eschatological sign," serving to remind those who take time to notice that this person witnesses to life and love beyond anything available in our present life on earth. Celibacy is also an organizing principle for life in a religious community; without it, there could be no Jesuit community life. But the rationale for celibacy runs even deeper than that.

When I was a young Jesuit, I was surprised to hear a recently ordained Jesuit priest remark that celibacy does no one any good except the celibate. That just didn't sound right to me at the time; you will understand why as you read further in this chapter.

The Jesuits' 34th General Congregation addressed the relationship of celibacy to community in 1995: "It is not that the community compensates for a wife and children, but rather that it can and
does support a life that is lived in their denial. Through the many
forms of their mutual presence to one another and their invest-
ment of themselves in one another's lives, Jesuits mediate to each
other the presence of that Lord to whom they have offered themselves through their vow of chastity. . . . The apostolic chastity of
a Jesuit cannot be lived in an aloof withdrawal from others. As a
true 'gift from above,' apostolic chastity should lead to communion
both with one's brother Jesuits and with the people we serve."[1]

The Church, as we all know, has for many centuries been
choosing her priests exclusively from men called to celibacy (and
that isn't likely to change any time soon). But Jesuit brothers—
men whose vocation is to service in the Society of Jesus but not
to priestly service—are also celibate. So celibacy has something
to do with the Jesuit way of life that is more than just the practical
availability normally associated with *priestly* celibacy.

Every year during Holy Week, the Chrism Mass is celebrated by
the diocesan bishop in his cathedral in the presence of his priests.
It gives them all a chance to think about celibate priesthood and
the paschal mystery. My personal reflcection on these mysteries is
aided by words from the pen of the late German Jesuit theologian
Karl Rahner:

> The priest is not an angel sent from heaven.
>
> He is a man, a member of the Church, a Christian.
>
> Remaining man and Christian, he begins to speak to you
> the word of God.
>
> This word is not his own. No, he comes to you because
> God has told him to proclaim God's word.
>
> Perhaps he has not entirely understood it himself. Perhaps
> he adulterates it. Perhaps he falters and stammers. How else
> could he speak God's word, ordinary man that he is?

> But must not some one of us say something about God,
> about eternal life, about the majesty of grace in our sancti-
> fied being; must not some one of us speak of sin, the judg-
> ment and mercy of God?²

Most friends and lay colleagues of Jesuit priests would have no difficulty seeing the men they know and admire in Rahner's description. But they have to look through the man to the mystery behind
his vocation to get some sense of the meaning of celibacy in his
life. That's the challenge in understanding the life of any priest.

The Mystery of Suffering

For the Christian, the issue of bad things happening to good people
raises the riddle of the paschal mystery. For priests, the questions
of human suffering and death are a daily challenge; they are men
who are called upon "to say something about God, about eternal
life, about the mystery of grace in our sanctified being." They've
got to say something that makes sense to good people when bad
things happen to them.

There was a wonderful Sulpician priest by the name of Gene
Walsh, whom I knew many years ago. He was fond of remind-
ing people that "Jesus promises you two things—your life will
have meaning, and you're going to live forever. If you can get a
better offer, take it." In that remark, Gene Walsh was making a
powerful point about God, grace, and eternal life. The "meaning"
Jesus gives to every human life is spelled out in the language of
mystery, the paschal mystery, and that is the mystery that sheds
some light on celibacy.

Holy Week provides us Christians with a special perspective
on our personal limitations, disappointments, failures, suffer-
ings, and eventual death. We are a people of hope, we Christians,
and we priests have to be witnesses to hope. Our Catholic people
expect us to have something to say to them in their difficulties.

Our Catholic people expect us to live the gospel we preach, a mysterious gospel of finding through losing, gaining by giving, winning through surrendering, and living by dying.

Rabbi Harold Kushner's book *When Bad Things Happen to Good People* is written from the heart of a deeply religious man whose son, Aaron, was diagnosed in infancy as having a condition called progeria, "rapid aging." He would only grow to be about three feet tall, have no hair on head or body, have the appearance of a little old man, and die in his early teen years. Speaking of his son in the introduction to this book, Rabbi Kushner writes, "This is his book because any attempt to make sense of the world's pain and evil will be judged a success or failure based on whether it offers an acceptable explanation of why he and we [his parents and sister] had to undergo what we did." [3]

Toward the end of his book, Rabbi Kushner writes:

> Let me suggest that the bad things that happen to us in our lives do not have a meaning when they happen to us. They do not happen for any good reason which would cause us to accept them willingly. But we can give them a meaning. We can redeem these tragedies from senselessness by imposing meaning on them. The question we should be asking is not, "Why did this happen to me? What did I do to deserve this?" That is really an unanswerable, pointless question. A better question would be "Now that this has happened to me, what am I going to do about it?" [4]

As I read those words, I wondered what meaning a specifically Christian spirituality might impose on them. Is there a Christian perspective, I asked myself, that might enlarge the interpretative framework needed to figure these things out? I wondered, from my Christian point of view, whether some "bad things" (the crucifixion of Jesus, for example) might not "have a meaning" when they happen. They could indeed, I found myself thinking, be accepted willingly for a very good theological reason, not for the bad reason that I would dismiss along with Kushner, namely, that something anyone did makes him or her deserve the bad outcome. That kind of thinking turns God into some kind of mean-spirited umpire anxious to call you "out" at the plate instead of eagerly waiting, as the father of the prodigal son in Luke's Gospel parable waited, to welcome you home.

Both Jewish spirituality and Christian spirituality are careful not to blame God when reversals occur. So-called acts of God are really acts of nature. True, God is the creator of all things natural, but nature's laws—the aging process or the law of gravity, for example—play out without divine interference. Kushner is particularly good on this point:

> I would say that God may not prevent the calamity, but He gives us the strength and the perseverance to overcome it. Where else do we get these qualities which we did not have before? The heart attack which slows down a forty-six-year-old businessman does not come from God, but the determination to change his life-style, to stop smoking, to care less about expanding the business and care more about spending time with his family, because his eyes have been opened to what is truly important to him—those things come from God. God does not stand for heart attacks; those are nature's responses to the body's being overstressed. But God does stand for self-discipline and for being part of a family.
>
> The flood that devastates a town is not an "act of God," even if the insurance companies find it useful to call it that. But the efforts people make to save lives, risking their own lives for a person who might be a total stranger to them, and the determination to rebuild their community after the flood waters have receded, do qualify as acts of God.
>
> When a person is dying of cancer, I do not hold God responsible for the cancer or for the pain he feels. They have other causes. But I have seen God give such people

the strength to take each day as it comes, to be grateful for a day full of sunshine or one in which they are relatively free of pain.[5]

Kushner acknowledges that these difficult questions will surface in every life and recur in every generation. "The questions never change; the search for a satisfying answer continues."[6] That is where I found myself pausing to reflect on this wonderful book and saying to myself, "No, for me the search has ended in Christ." The reflective Christian, I believe, has met Christ as a serious questioner meets a satisfying answer. Christian spirituality savors the satisfaction of the answer in a challenging, but never complacent, way.

The challenge is what Christians call the paschal mystery. Before exploring that mystery and its link to celibacy, I want to associate myself with one final excerpt from Rabbi Kushner's book. Any person of faith, Jew or Christian, could agree with this:

> Is there an answer to the question of why bad things happen to good people? That depends on what we mean by "answer." If we mean "is there an explanation which will make sense of it all?"—why is there cancer in the world? Why did my father get cancer? Why did the plane crash? Why did my child die?—then there is probably no satisfying answer. We can offer learned explanations, but in the end, when we have covered all the squares on the game board and are feeling very proud of our cleverness, the pain and the anguish and the sense of unfairness will still be there.[7]

But, I have to remind myself, so will I "still be there," and what will I have to say—to myself or anyone who turns to me for help? Life goes on, and life will be there challenging me to get on with it, to face up to the future, to help others, to love and smile and grow, and to believe that God is there with me, right at my side, just as I assure the believer that God is there with him or her in anguished moments of suffering and loss.

In Galatians 5:22 is a lineup of qualities that I like to call the Pauline criteria for the presence of the Spirit. Paul calls them the fruit of the Holy Spirit: love, joy, peace, patience, kindness, generosity, faithfulness, gentleness, self-control. These qualities make up the infrastructure of a functioning spirituality. They provide invisible means of support. They are "soft" qualities in the eyes of the world; I think of them as elements of a slingshot spirituality that can be carried into a hard, cold world. The slingshot worked well for David against Goliath. Admittedly, this slingshot spirituality equips the Christian with soft solutions to life's hard problems.[8] But it can give balance, coherence, and consistency to a believer's life.

Celibacy and the Paschal Mystery

Belief in Jesus as Messiah and Son of God sets us Christians apart from Jews at the foundation of our faith. And the difference lies not simply in an assent, on the part of Christians, to the proposition that Jesus is divine; the difference will work itself out in a spirituality that integrates, however incompletely, the dimensions of the paschal mystery. Notice the echo of the paschal mystery in the opening prayer in the special Mass we have for the sick:

> Father, your son accepted our sufferings to teach us the virtue of patience in human illness. Hear the prayers we offer for our sick brothers and sisters. May all who suffer pain, illness, or disease realize that they are chosen to be saints, and know that they are joined to Christ in his sufferings for the salvation of the world.[9]

"For the salvation of the world." Out of the suffering comes salvation. And the suffering becomes an instrument in human hands to work with Christ for the salvation of the world. There is an enormous amount of relevance in all of this to the call to celibacy. God calls men to priesthood, and part of that reality is the call to celibacy.

Whatever the controversy over priestly celibacy in the Church today, care must be taken not to lose appreciation for the way that celibacy participates in the mystery of the grain of wheat, which, of course, is part of the basic message of the gospel. As Jesus teaches in the Gospel of John, "Unless a grain of wheat falls to the ground and dies, it remains just a grain of wheat; but if it dies, it produces much fruit" (12:24). The "death" of celibacy brings forth life; it is fruitful. There is reproduction in the order of grace. Celibacy does a lot of good for the celibate and for countless others as well.

There is, as we know, an apostolic celibacy that has a practical, measurable purpose. It is functional, intended to facilitate priestly service. There is also totally gratuitous celibacy, a mystery for which there is no fully satisfying explanation. You have to try to locate that celibacy within the paschal mystery.

All of us Christians, clergy and lay, are beneficiaries of the paschal mystery. Christ died and rose so that we might live. For us, there is life through his death. We priests die the death of celibacy, and others rise. We rise too, but we benefit others who, because of our sacrifice, are renewed in grace. All analogies limp, but I find this one helpful: You walk into a room and flip a switch on the wall. Lights come on, but you rarely give a thought to the source of that light. There is a power generator somewhere unknown to you that provides you with light. I firmly believe that our celibacy, in God's gracious providence, generates power in the order of grace for others. I believe that there is reproduction in the order of grace because of committed and dedicated celibates.

I like to think of the donation of celibacy. The given life draws God's favor on the community, not just on the celibate. The grain of wheat left to itself produces nothing. Only when it appears to have died and has been buried does it bring forth fruit. We Jesuits are called to this kind of a given, celibate life; we're not called to bachelorhood. And the given life, as we readily preach to others, is the happy life. We must be concerned, of course, about witnessing to this. We have to show evidence of being happy men doing useful work—happy men in and through whom there is reproduction in the order of grace. Sure, there will be loneliness at times, but celibacy makes the celibate a crowd of one whose life enlivens unknown others spiritually.

I cherish this faith-based reflection of Cardinal John Henry Newman; it speaks to me of the value of celibacy:

> God has created me to do Him some definite service; He has committed some work to me which He has not committed to another. I have my mission—I may never know it in this life, but I shall be told it in the next.
>
> I am a link in a chain, a bond of connection between persons. He has not created me for nothing. I shall do good; I shall do His work. I shall be an angel of peace, a preacher of truth in my own place while not intending it—if I do but keep His commandments.
>
> Therefore, I will trust Him, whatever, wherever, I am. I can never be thrown away. If I am in sickness, my sickness may serve him; in perplexity, my perplexity may serve Him; if I am in sorrow, my sorrow may serve Him. He does nothing in vain. He knows what He is about. He may take away my friends, He may throw me among strangers, He may make me feel desolate, make my spirits sink, hide my future from me—still He knows what He is about.[10]

He knows what he is about when he calls men and women to celibacy.

It is easy to recall during Holy Week that the Jesus of history no longer exists as he is portrayed in the Gospels and as we follow him devotionally on the Way of the Cross. The Jesus of history is a memory. The glorified Jesus, the victorious Jesus, lives now in glory. He is an eternal winner. He is with the Church now. His victory can never be reversed. There is no smug complacency in our knowledge of this victory. It is not so much that we have picked a winner but that a winner has picked us! And the good news of the paschal mystery is there to be proclaimed through the witness of celibacy all year long.

Celibacy and Sexuality

Before closing out this reflection on celibacy, it is only fair, I think, to take a moment to address the question that some friends and colleagues of Jesuits might have but would be too polite to ask. For some of our lay associates it is more curiosity than question. It relates to sexual orientation, and the question will be raised by friends, gay and straight, who want to know more about the Society.

I'd like first to say simply that all Jesuits are called to celibacy. That is the really important thing; that is a fundamental issue to be discerned when considering the Jesuit life. Both heterosexual and homosexual men who are prepared to commit themselves to celibacy can, if God calls them, have a place in the Society of Jesus. One's sexual orientation is not the important issue; the successful integration of one's sexuality into a balanced and holy life is. And regardless of orientation, willingness to live one's life in fidelity to the demands of the vow of chastity is an essential predisposition for anyone considering the Jesuit vocation.

Jesuits of either sexual orientation have and will continue to emerge as advocates for the civil, economic, political, and human rights of homosexuals; that is part of the modern Jesuit commitment to the promotion of justice. Given the discrimination faced on a daily basis by gays and lesbians, there is a pressing need for the promotion of justice in their regard. In this as in all other questions of justice, Jesuit advocacy, if it is to be faithfully and genuinely Jesuit, will always be consistent with the principles of Catholic moral theology. Jesuit advocacy for homosexual rights, if it is to be authentically Jesuit, will reflect the Society's charism and commitment to thinking with the Church.

It should be acknowledged that there have been behavioral lapses with respect to celibacy—relatively few, but lapses nonetheless—on the part of both hetero- and homosexual Jesuits, some quite young, others who have lived the life for many years. Human weakness is one thing, understandable, even though regrettable; but the violation of integrity—presenting oneself as a man of the vows when one's behavior gives the lie to that impression—is quite another. Forgiveness is available to all, but the Jesuit life, as Ignatius wrote of it in the Constitutions, presumes commitment and recommitment to a very high standard. "What pertains to the vow of chastity," wrote Ignatius, "requires no interpretation, since it is evident how perfectly it should be preserved, by endeavoring to imitate therein the purity of the angels in cleanness of body and mind" (*Const*, 547).[11]

Some of the interpretation that Ignatius thought to be unnecessary was provided nonetheless by the 34th General Congregation in its Complementary Norms to the Constitutions:

> By the vow of chastity, we devote ourselves to the Lord and to his service in such a unique love that it excludes marriage and any other exclusive human relationship, as well as the genital expression and gratification of sexuality. Thus the vow entails the obligation of complete continence in celibacy for the sake of the kingdom of heaven. Following the evangelical counsel of chastity, we aspire to deepen our familiarity with God, our configuration to Christ, our companionship with our brother Jesuits, our service to our neighbors whoever they may be; and at the same time we aspire to grow in our personal maturity and capacity to love. (*CN*, 144)

No one ever said it was going to be easy. But the love on which the entire commitment is based can make it a joy. How can this be? The answer lies in faith. My faith convinces me that the Jesuit celibate is a crowd of one whose celibacy empowers him to do more good than he will, this side of heaven, ever know.

The love involved in celibacy is, of course, first and foremost love for Jesus Christ. "The only real motivation for celibacy," said Cardinal Godfried Daneels of Belgium, speaking to an audience of seminary rectors at Louvain University in August 1998, "is being faithful to the total imitation of Jesus Christ. . . . Celibacy is an issue of love, and love cannot be explained or reasoned. . . . The why and wherefore of celibate love for Christ is celibate love for Christ. It cannot be explained further than that."

I don't presume to be able to explain it further, but as I say amen to the words of Cardinal Daneels, I want to add an alleluia that comes when I apply to the sacrifice of celibacy these words of Dorothy Day: "The consolation is this and this our faith too: By our suffering and our failures, by our acceptance of the Cross, we unleash forces that help to overcome the evil in the world."[12] That's what I mean by reproduction in the order of grace. That's what makes the celibate a crowd of one.

CHAPTER 9

Individuarians

Jesuits are individuarians. The word is not in the dictionary, at least not yet. It is one I employ to describe men who are neither rugged individualists nor ideological communists, even though they are strong-minded individuals (you can always tell a Jesuit, but you can't tell him much!) whose vow of poverty necessarily commits them to a common life.

Commun*ism* is an inappropriate doctrine for Jesuits, and individual*ism* is not a concept that fairly describes their spirit and spirituality. The typical Jesuit simply does not fit into a description or definition like the following:

> Individualists, as the name implies, are not trying to create a community but rather aiming to free themselves from the fetters of social restriction. They thrive in loose organizational structures, around which they can move freely without long-term commitment, able to negotiate their own dealings with other individuals. Well-being for them means the freedom to pursue self-interested ends. It is the well-being of the narrowly defined ego, the ideal of negative freedom from interference.[1]

I'm not suggesting that no Jesuit ever fit that description; I'm simply saying that most Jesuits have higher ideals, larger hearts, and wider horizons.

Just as *communitarian* is a label that came into currency several decades ago to describe a socially responsible, environmentally sensitive, free-enterprising outlook, *individuarian* now seems useful in categorizing Jesuits. It provides me with a label that sets my subject (Jesuits in general) apart from the individual of the psychologist and the collectivity of the sociologist, without losing sight of the uniquely personal character of any Jesuit vocation.

Jesuits are contemplatives in action; they take their monasteries with them as they immerse themselves in the world. Their apostolic formation

> must favor the personal assimilation of Christian experience, an experience that is spiritual, personal, vital, rooted in faith, nourished by daily prayer and the Eucharist; an experience that makes [them] capable of cooperating with God for the spiritual growth of believers and of communicating the gift of faith to nonbelievers. (*CN*, 65)

Official Jesuit formation policy also states, "Great care should be taken to direct each one according to his own gifts, both natural and spiritual. At the same time a sense of solidarity and collaboration should be fostered and every trace of egoism removed" (*CN*, 73). The developing Jesuit is formed to emerge as a balanced person ready to live an active life bordered by the personal and the communal, an individual in community. That's what I mean by the term *individuarian*.

Jesuits take a vow of obedience but are expected to be self-starting apostles whose lives are characterized by availability, flexibility, and willingness to work anywhere in the world for the greater glory of God. Their religious order encourages them to develop their intellectual gifts to the highest level of professional credentialing so that they can mix comfortably in the secular world of ideas and influence, a world where Jesuits simply cannot move in packs. They are to give freely what they have freely received. They live within rules but without geographic boundaries.

A High-Hearted Love of Christ

Few, if any, twentieth-century Jesuits were as comfortable in the world of ideas and culture as was the influential theologian John Courtney Murray. It was in a speech of his that I found these words of the German Jesuit Peter Lippert, words that help me see something compellingly individuarian in the Jesuit vocation faithfully lived: "The Society formally lives on its trust in each of its members. Each day in their life is a hundredfold appeal to their independent and energetic sense of duty, to their free good will, to their high-hearted love of Christ."

Father Murray was speaking in 1944 at the seventy-fifth anniversary of Woodstock College, the Jesuit theological seminary in Maryland where he taught and wrote for many years. The man he was quoting entered the Society in 1899 and worked as a writer, radio commentator, frequent contributor to *Stimmen der Zeit*, and author of several books. Peter Lippert died at age fifty-seven in 1937; John Murray died at age sixty-four in 1967.

The Society of Jesus quite literally lives on the trust it places in all of its members, the great, like Murray and Lippert, and the not so great; it encourages initiative and expects accountability. And there lies a clue to understanding these individuarians that go by the name Jesuit.

Another clue is rooted in Scripture. James Agee, who wrote *Time* magazine's August 20, 1945, cover story on the end of World War II, used Scripture to make this important point:

> When the bomb split open the universe and revealed the prospect of the infinitely extraordinary, it also revealed the oldest, simplest, commonest, most neglected and most important of facts: that each man is eternally and above all else responsible for his own soul, and in the terrible words of the Psalmist, that no man may deliver his brother, nor make agreement unto God for him.

Personal accountability before God is a nontransferable responsibility that dates back to the dawn of creation; there is something good and deep and unavoidable in the Jesuit spirit that I'm identifying here as individuarian.

Jesuit governance is rooted in what the order calls the "account of conscience." *Fortune*, the business magazine, pointed out many years ago that accountability in the business context of performance evaluation "all started with Loyola."

In the rule of life Ignatius drew up for his men, every Jesuit is expected to have an in-depth conversation with his provincial superior and his local superior once a year. It is called the "manifestation" or "account of conscience" to indicate an opening up, a self-disclosure, a willingness to be known by the one who governs so that, knowing all his men in this way, he (the superior) can govern better.

It is not uncommon now to call this an "apostolic conversation," a term that better catches the positive purpose of the exchange. The superior listens; the individual Jesuit talks about his strengths and weaknesses, his fears and achievements, his highs and lows, his dreams and disappointments, his forward motion in the spiritual life as well as his slippages and setbacks. In effect, the Jesuit, in the presence of his superior, is locating himself as best he can while he stands before a loving God, who called him to and sustains him in his apostolic vocation.

Peter Lippert's observation that the Society "lives on its trust" in its individual members leaves unsaid what every Jesuit knows, namely, that the Society expects accountability. It is always difficult for the superior, as it is for the parent of an adolescent, to know where trust ends and neglect begins. The superior, however, is not a parent, and the individual Jesuit is surely not an adolescent. Nonetheless, it is always possible for a superior to shirk his responsibility and for any Jesuit to avoid accountability. Rugged individualists might choose the avoidance route; individuarians are far less likely to do so.

Let me close out this discussion of Jesuit accountability with these words from the Complementary Norms to the Constitutions, published in 1996:

> The account of conscience, by which the superior becomes able to take part in each one's discernment and to help him therein, is to retain intact its value and vitality as an element of great moment in the spiritual governance of the Society. Therefore, all should give an account of conscience to their superiors, according to the norms and spirit of the Society, inspired by charity, with any obligation under pain of sin always precluded. In addition, the relationships between superiors and their brethren in the Society should be such as to encourage the manifestation of conscience and conversation about spiritual matters.
>
> No one, without exception, may directly or indirectly make known what has been revealed in an account of conscience unless it is with the express consent of the one rendering the account. (*CN*, 155)

Confidentiality is guaranteed; coercion is explicitly ruled out. It is adult and practical, free and spiritual. And it works for the growth of the individual and the progress of the whole.

Some Jesuits are never around, if the complaint of those who seem to be always around is to be believed. Some are not around at times for good apostolic reasons; some are among the missing for reasons that have little to do with zeal. It is best not to judge (and thus count on not being judged on this point!), but Jesuits have to deal with this issue.

The Being and the Doing of Jesuit Life

Our life is a life of balance (some may see it as a chosen form of imbalance given our vowed commitment to poverty, chastity, and obedience, but we are, for the most part, healthy, happy men living balanced religious lives). We have to balance the *being* and the *doing* of our vocation, called, as we are, to life in apostolic communities. We have chosen something quite different from the intimacy of the conjugal community, which is not to say that we have chosen a cold, impersonal, barrackslike existence. We are not only religious men comfortable with a necessary degree of solitude but also intellectual men who need quiet time for study and related pursuits. As teachers, many of us are touched by a cultural problem that besets the teaching profession. Educational theorist Stephen D. Brookfield makes the negative judgment in his book *Becoming a Critically Reflective Teacher* that the teaching culture on many college campuses today is characterized by "silence, individualism, and secrecy." Jesuit instructors, teachers, and professors are not altogether immune to that cultural virus, but most have developed strong resistance to it by making themselves open to out-of-classroom contact with students, collaborating with lay colleagues in service and research projects, and showing hospitality to students and faculty friends.

Moreover, we Jesuits, regardless of where we work, are at the service of others who can make proper, but unpredictable, demands on our time (it will be ever thus if we are committed to helping souls). So we are often going to be alone either in community preparing to be of help or apart from community individually serving others.

Balanced against all this is the sharing, in "union of minds and hearts," of our lives with other Jesuits in community, where we worship, pray, dine, relax, converse, and experience companionship and from where we often go out in pairs or small groups for a good time together.

Those who work in what the Society calls "formation"—the spiritual and intellectual preparation of young Jesuits for the apostolate—and those who are active in the recruitment of candidates for the Jesuit life note that young men entering the Society today have a pronounced interest in community. They want to *be* together in communities of shared spirituality. This is not to say that they are uninterested in *doing* apostolic works for the love of Christ; it simply points to an interest in finding companionship in community. "Candidates know we are strong individuals," remarked one vocation director, "but they want to know how these strong individuals relate to one another."

In a remarkably perceptive article about changing attitudes toward the relationship between life and work in contemporary religious communities, especially newly emerging communities, Patricia Wittberg, SC, notes that the role of religious communities has "shifted from providing an institutional setting for ministerial service to facilitating the individualized ministries of its members. . . . Increasingly, people enter religious life or stay in it for the spiritual and communal benefits they can gain from their membership, not to perform ministerial works."[2] They perform ministerial works, of course, but individually, and often not in institutions sponsored by their religious order.

Jesuits have always had their lone rangers, talented and zealous men on solo flights. The Society also has many good community men whose work in the apostolate remains unobserved and in some cases unknown by those with whom they pray and dine back in the community at day's end. It is clear, however, that today's Jesuits of all ages are now more interested in learning from one another details about the work they do as well as the faith they share.

Unusual If Not Unique

It is important to note that Jesuits live in a worldwide community, having a lot in common with men from diverse nations and cultures. They also live in a province community in a way that I will illustrate below. Of course, they live in local communities of varying sizes, shapes, and levels of interpersonal commitment. The Jesuits and their schools are at once local, regional, national, and international, and in this the order is surely unusual, if not unique.

I think a bell curve is useful in defining the community relationship (and from a practical point of view, the financial dependency) of an individual Jesuit from his novitiate through his retirement from full-time ministry. Formation years mean financial dependency on the province. There is no tuition charge, no "dowry," no payment of any kind required of an entrant into the Society of Jesus. (If he chooses to leave the Society, there is no compensation for services rendered, no severance package, except for an appropriate cash grant to assist him in his transition back to lay life.)

A Jesuit's active apostolic years mean financial dependency on the local community for meals and wheels, health care, clothes, books, and other typical expenses. The local community, in turn, is dependent on income from the apostolate.

From novitiate until regency (the name for a period of two or three years when study is interrupted in favor of direct apostolic work), the scholastic is financially dependent on the province. A regent receives financial support from the local community, but he contributes to it by working in the assigned apostolate, usually teaching in one of our schools. Theological training, tertianship (a third year of novitiate-like emphasis on prayer and the spiritual life), and special graduate studies for those so assigned mean a return to full financial dependency on the province.

Once formed and finished with studies, the Jesuit becomes financially dependent on a local community. This stage is represented by the rising, or elevated, portion of the bell curve, which will turn down eventually as he moves toward retirement. Once retired (at any age), the Jesuit may return to financial dependency on the province, although it is common for a man to remain as most welcome, supported by, and fully appreciated in the community where he lived during his active and compensated years.

The left side, or beginning, of the bell curve is sharply defined for all Jesuits; a sharper definition is now developing on the right.

For example, I can look back and see myself on the left side of the bell curve during my early Jesuit years in the familiar old categories of novice, junior, philosopher, and theologian (all periods of the formative years). I think now of new and unnamed categories ahead of me on the other side of the curve, on the downside. I think of those of us who are over seventy as seniors. In the case of some seniors who become frail or infirm and are missioned to pray for the Church and the Society, I like to imagine them (and myself when I get there) as companions of the Lord. A sense of this special companionship was caught, I think, in the following words of our late Father General Pedro Arrupe (1907–91) during his final illness: "More than ever I find myself in the hands of God. This is what I have wanted all my life from my youth. But now there is a difference; the initiative is entirely with God. It is indeed a profound spiritual experience to know and feel myself so totally in God's hands."[3]

During our Jesuit formation and actively apostolic years, we are encouraged to think of ourselves as companions *in* the Lord; when that more active companionship fades, the Society's spirituality invites us, as Father Arrupe's words suggest, to become more conscious companions *of* the Lord. Although some of us might balk at being named seniors, who could possibly resent being called a companion of the Lord?

Meanwhile, there's a lot of work to be done, and Jesuits will find themselves doing it *ad majorem Dei gloriam* in pairs, packs, or solo flights. They will do it in institutions that are owned and operated by Jesuits, in works founded by Jesuits but now managed by laypeople and owned by independent boards of trustees, and in institutions with no relationship at all to the Society of Jesus. Moreover, and most interesting of all, some Jesuits will do effective work without any institutional base whatever. And Ignatius would warmly approve all of the above! He would also approve, I think, any signs among Jesuits of what Robert Bellah calls "expressive individualism."

As a practical man, however (a practical genius, some would say), Ignatius wrote the Constitutions to structure his order's way of proceeding, and most of his followers will find it congenial to work within structured settings. I've often remarked that without a bone structure, I'd be a puddle of flesh on the floor; similarly, without an institutional structure, my Jesuit work might well be a shapeless mass of good intentions with little impact and no lasting effect.

There are generational differences in the Society of Jesus today about the size and style of community, the right balance between being and doing together, the amount of energy invested in turning toward one another in support and sharing, as contrasted with turning out toward those we want to serve. We used to walk to meals and prayer in a long, black line; black cassocks were worn at home and on the job in rectories, classrooms, and other places in our institutions. When we left the house, we wore black suits and Roman collars.

Few Jesuits own a cassock anymore. On the street they are often indistinguishable by dress from their lay colleagues and the laity they serve in the apostolate. Some who respect symbols and think it helpful to have a differentiating characteristic wear a lapel pin that bears an imprint of the seal of the Society of Jesus; this pin marks them as religious and members of the Jesuit order.

Common Life

Our rule instructs us that the "manner is ordinary" with respect to meals, dress, housing, and the externals of our religious life together. Tensions arise now and then with respect to personal use of cars. No one in the Society owns anything outright, so car ownership is not the issue. Exclusive personal use of a car, even when it is clearly part of the tool kit needed to do a job, can inject a troublesome "haves against have-nots" atmosphere. This problem is not solved by the widespread use of a sign-out reservation sheet for the use of community cars available to all. Some neglect to return the cars on time, and others forget to put the keys back on the hook. Some mistake E on the gas gauge for "Enough" when they return the car. Others use invisible ink or illegible handwriting on the sign-out sheet in anticipation of a fender bender that will go unreported when the car is back on the lot. And so it goes. Many large families could relate the same scenario. So what else is new? By the way, doesn't the automobile symbolize better than just about anything else in America the individualism that is so widespread in the broader culture? Surely Jesuits are not untouched by that culture, even as they try to live their lives as vowed religious in a consciously countercultural way.

I was introduced to the Jesuit life by Father John V. McEvoy, SJ, who served from about 1939 to 1951 as the master of novices, or "Father Master," for several hundred newcomers to the Maryland Province of the Society of Jesus. Our novitiate was located in Wernersville, Pennsylvania. One summer evening after a cookout and several hours of recreation in a grove at the edge of the novitiate grounds, Father McEvoy gave about forty of us novices "points" for the next morning's meditation. He highlighted the Latin phrase *justus ut palma florebit* in verse 13 of Psalm 92. The words were familiar to us in those days of the Latin Mass; they served as the Introit verse for a Mass honoring holy men and women.

Just persons, the righteous ones, will "flourish like the palm tree," according to the psalmist, and they will grow "like a cedar of Lebanon."

> Planted in the house of the LORD,
>> they shall flourish in the courts of our God.
> They shall bear fruit even in old age,
>> always vigorous and sturdy. (Psalm 92:14–15)

There we were on the edge of Pennsylvania's Lebanon Valley, under the stars, preparing to pray the next morning about our call to be just men, to be upright like palm trees. Father McEvoy explained that just as palm trees always spread their roots to seek out water,

we should stretch our faith roots toward the sacramental source
of grace that is ours each day in the Eucharist. We should allow
ourselves, by God's grace, to become rooted. Rootedness in Christ
would be a special part of our Jesuit way of proceeding.

Justus ut palma florebit. We were invited to pray that we too
might "flourish in the courts of our God."

Since that night, I've always thought about the Jesuit ideal of
being like a palm tree planted in the direction of grace, not water.
So I was struck years later by the following footnote that accompa-
nies the first psalm in the New American Bible's 1991 edition. The
first psalm is, the note says,

> A preface to the whole Book of Psalms, contrasting with
> striking similes the destiny of the good and the wicked. The
> psalm views life as activity, as choosing either the good or
> the bad. Each "way" brings its inevitable consequences. The
> wise through their good actions will experience rootedness
> and life, and the wicked, rootlessness and death.

The first psalm speaks of those "who do not follow the counsel of
the wicked" as being "like a tree / planted near streams of water, /
that yields its fruit in season; / Its leaves never wither; / whatever
they do prospers" (verses 1, 3). It was in this spirit that Dr. Douglas
Horton, retired dean of the Harvard Divinity School, eulogized
Jesuit Father Gustave Weigel with these words: "Fixed as he was
in the things of eternity, he could sit loose to the things of time." I
find something remarkably and beautifully Jesuit in those ideas.

As I said at the beginning, Jesuits are individuarians, rooted
individuarians. They know that they cannot "make agreement
unto God" for one another. But they feel blessed to be called by
God to be together even if, in some cases, they go their separate
ways without the aid of wheels!

One former Jesuit, a classmate of mine who withdrew from the
seminary after ten years and is now a happily married father of five,
always repeats during our annual lunch and recollection of our

early Jesuit days, "It's the greatest outfit in the world." He means it. And he is at peace with the conviction that it simply wasn't the right outfit for him. He was neither sufficiently individuarian nor adequately communitarian to find his happiness as a Jesuit. But in spirit and outlook, like so many of those who will read this book, he is still one of us.

CHAPTER 10

Stewardship: The Jesuit Approach to the Use of Wealth, Power, and Talent

In 1975 I wrote a small book called *Toward Stewardship*, which is now out of print. I'm not sure what prompted me to write it or what led me to reflect on the richness of the biblical, even prebiblical, concept of stewardship. I was teaching social ethics to Jesuits at Woodstock College, a theological school, at that time, and I found the notion of stewardship to be a useful category as I tried to get at the underpinnings of the moral arguments related to certain issues of social ethics, namely, the poverty gap, environmental pollution, and the maldistribution and abuse of power in the human community. So I called the book *Toward Stewardship* and added the subtitle *An Interim Ethic of Poverty, Pollution, and Power.*[1]

Now, many years later, I want to take another look at the idea of stewardship and use it as an interpretative category to explain the Jesuit approach to wealth, power, and talent. It is neither misreading history nor boasting to point out that there has been a lot of Jesuit talent in service to the Church over the past five centuries and that possessors of that talent have also enjoyed a good deal of influence in both ecclesiastical and civil societies. Moreover, Jesuits have a way of turning up from time to time in circles where the wealthy gather, and most of the time they are there for a very good purpose.

117

It might be useful to begin with a reminder that the idea of stewardship has been around for quite a while, long before the Jesuits appeared on the scene. Many modern Catholics tend to regard it as a Protestant concept unrelated to the core of their Catholic commitment, but that is simply not the case. And many Protestants tend to associate stewardship with support of their local congregations and with pastoral accountability for the use of funds. Those are worthy objectives but are far from the full explanation of the meaning of stewardship.

The central idea of stewardship is simply this: wealth possessed is held in trust for others. The possession of wealth involves responsibilities beyond the self; the greater the wealth, the more awesome the responsibility.

The first verse of Psalm 24 makes the simple faith assertion "The earth is the Lord's, and the fulness thereof" (KJV). Everything—the earth and all it yields or holds in hidden deposits—is the Lord's. And so is "the fulness thereof"—all that is cultivated, extracted, fabricated, or in any way developed from that original given, the earth. Fenders and furniture, homes and hyacinths—all are owned by God. We may have legal title and regard ourselves accordingly as owners. But we should understand that we are users, not owners; we are caretakers, not controllers. We (by "we" I mean all of us in the human race, not just Jesuits) manage property that is not our own, no matter what the title papers say.

In the book of Leviticus, you'll find the Lord speaking to Moses on Mount Sinai and instructing him to tell the Israelites that "the land belongs to me, and to me you are only strangers and guests" (25:23, JB). The idea of stewardship incorporates this guest relationship, which characterizes those of us on the land who are entrusted with wealth that belongs to God. We own nothing absolutely; we are stewards. As St. Paul remarks in 1 Corinthians 4:2, "What is expected of stewards is that each one should be found worthy of his [or her] trust" (JB).

This notion of stewardship applies to all believers; every last one of us is absolutely dependent on a Creator-God. Stewardship should be a spiritual reality and moral category that affects the behavior of any believer. There is nothing uniquely or even characteristically Jesuit about this notion; it is simply useful in understanding the Jesuit way of managing this world's goods and gifts.

For centuries, the Catholic theological tradition has understood the *use* of property to be common (and this by divine plan), while the *ownership* of property may be private (as the best accommodation to the fallen state of sinful human nature).

"Like Good Stewards"

Christian theology can give no better answer to questions about use and ownership of property than St. Peter gave when he wrote, "Above all, never let your love for each other grow insincere, since love covers over many a sin. Welcome each other into your houses without grumbling. Each one of you has received a special grace, so, like good stewards responsible for all these different graces of God, put yourselves at the service of others" (1 Peter 4:8–10, JB). To share "without grumbling" seems to be the demand that the idea of stewardship places upon followers of Christ. Sharing can take many forms; so can ownership and stewardship.

Clement of Alexandria wrote a treatise titled *The Rich Man's Salvation* and asked in chapter 13, "What society could exist on earth, if no one owned anything?" "None" is the literal answer to that question taken literally. Although ownership is, as common sense and the Christian tradition affirm, both necessary and natural, the Jesuit vow of poverty establishes a society—the Society of Jesus—where no one Jesuit owns anything. (The Society does, through its central government and provincial and local community corporations, hold title to significant quantities of land, buildings, equipment, and financial assets.) The individual Jesuit has a net worth of zero. He has the use of money and property necessary to do his job. He has a body to care for and a mind to develop; thus, like any Christian owner, he has to ask himself, "How do I handle my ownership responsibilities in light of what the gospel of Christ calls me to be?" The answer to that question is stewardship.

Jesuits are always talking about the *magis*, a Latin word for "more" that appears in the text of Ignatius' *Spiritual Exercises* and is repeated throughout Jesuit literature. Their motto, *ad majorem Dei gloriam,* drives Jesuits to do well anything that they do and to do it for the greater glory of God. The *magis* represents the spirit of Jesuit stewardship applied to the use of talent or any tools needed for the apostolate.

Jesuit stewardship relates primarily to immaterial possessions. Intellectual gifts are abundant in the Society; their potential is developed generously to impressive levels of competence both by men who are willing to study and by a Society that is willing to pay the bills. Geniuses are relatively few in our ranks, but generous men familiar with the asceticism of disciplined academic work are plentiful. Not all these talented men pursue academic careers, but wherever they work they bring to the task well-trained minds as well as generous hearts. Moreover, not a few Jesuits are men of modest intellectual gifts who understand that excelling (pursuing the *magis*) means making a significant advance from a well-defined starting point. God gives the starting point; God's grace impels the cooperating Jesuit to excel. Many choose to excel at teaching. They are the schoolmasters who have touched and continue to touch the lives of students all over the world. Both teaching and studying are exercises of stewardship.

For centuries, the Jesuit way of proceeding has been putting a premium on the intellect. This is responsible stewardship and is not likely to change.

Charlie Shreiner, a friend of mine since our college days together at St. Joseph's in Philadelphia, made an interesting observation to me from his later perspective as a faculty member and administrator at his alma mater. "You Jesuits are five-percenters," he remarked. "You tend to become preoccupied with the 5 percent you don't have and are insufficiently appreciative of the 95 percent that is clearly yours." He was speaking of Jesuit talent, competence, and apostolic results in the world of ideas.

I thought of that remark when I read a *New York Times* review of *Cyril Connolly: A Life* by Jeremy Lewis.

> Although the distinguished English critic and editor Cyril Connolly played a leading role in English literary life from the 1930's until his death in 1974, he seldom lived up to his own uncompromising standards. In fact, to judge by [this] surprisingly candid authorized biography, Connolly was accurate when he described himself as a "lazy irresolute person, over-vain and over-modest, unsure in my judgments and unable to finish what I have begun."[2]

Cyril Connolly was far from being a Jesuit, but not all Jesuits are far from this kind of self-appraisal. "He tended to look down on the highly polished essays, reviews and satires at which he excelled and which made up the bulk of his writings. Yet he managed to complete only one novel, and, perhaps fearful of not fulfilling his own promise, he abandoned any number of ambitious literary projects."[3]

Father C. J. McNaspy, a twentieth-century American Jesuit from the New Orleans Province, was well known as a musicologist, literary critic, teacher, editor, and author. When I greeted him on his sixtieth birthday, he told me that his fortieth had been more difficult for him to handle. He said, "I knew then that I would never do anything great, and now I'm quite adjusted to that."

The record, of course, shows otherwise. C. J., as we all called him, did many great things, touched the lives of thousands pastorally and academically, and wrote a bundle of books and articles. He responded generously at age sixty-five to his superior's request that he go to Paraguay to introduce young seminarians there to the classics, as he had done at Grand Coteau,

Louisiana, for the Jesuit scholastics in his own province decades earlier in his career. Both his talent and his modesty were summed up for me one day when, book in hand, he popped into my doorway (two down the hall from his) in the Jesuit faculty residence at Loyola University in New Orleans. He was a faculty member there at that time; I was his dean. C. J. wanted to share something from the open book and read it aloud for me. I noticed as he read without the slightest pause that he was translating from a French text as he went merrily along. When I commented on the smooth translation, he replied quite matter-of-factly and without the hint of a boast, "Oh yes, I guess I read French as well as anyone I know!"

Many of us come up short in our push for the *magis*; too many of us fail to appreciate the good work we do with the tools and talent that are ours. We're not proud of either failing. Nor are we proud of past failures to be better stewards of our bodily health. On this point, there are encouraging signs in medical statistics that Jesuits have been evangelized by the cholesterol-conscious, exercise-promoting, alcohol-moderating, antismoking secular society. By and large, we have gotten the moderation message and can mount as evidence of reform fewer strokes and heart attacks in our ranks.

The record is less clear (or at least the indicators are more difficult to read) with regard to the stewardship of the access we have to laypeople who clearly possess both wealth and power. We have educated many of them in our schools; we know others as parents of our students, parishioners in our urban parishes, or annual retreatants in our retreat houses and spirituality centers. Those schools, parishes, and retreat houses look to wealthy alumni, parents, and friends for needed support. You don't get that support without asking for it, and you can't ask someone you don't know and have made no effort to befriend. So mix we must with the rich and powerful, but much of that mixing is on behalf of the poor and powerless.

Middle-Class Moorings

In the Society, there is a good deal of conversation these days about lifestyle, and within a given province, comparisons are often made between higher education communities (the haves) and communities associated with secondary schools or parish apostolates (those presumed to be the have-nots). Often the comparative differences are a function of size and age of the buildings where we live; almost always there is a conscious effort on the part of Jesuits to avoid extremes and maintain a modest, median standard of living.

I once asked the legendary Father Horace McKenna, SJ, apostle to the poor and homeless in Washington, D.C., whether he thought we Jesuits should move closer to the radical kind of poverty that Dorothy Day espoused for her Catholic Worker movement.

"No," he replied. "We're middle class. We have to be there for the long haul, and we need middle-class moorings." (He had his at the Gonzaga High School Jesuit residence.)

Then, with his memory fixed on past efforts made to gain a better sense of solidarity with the poor, this saintly priest told me how he used to make his annual eight-day retreat in a homeless shelter. "You get the first two nights free," he explained, "and then I'd ask the minister [the official in his local Jesuit community who handled meals, wheels, and money] for the fifty cents a night I needed for the rest of the retreat." Horace McKenna was not typical, but he was not so unusual that he didn't fit in with the rest of his Jesuit brothers.

To keep it all in perspective (relative to both the preferential option for the poor that the Society wants to achieve and the Jesuit use of wealth, power, and talent that our vocation requires), examine the comparative economic status of Jesuit institutions in the broader higher education community. Compare, for example, Seattle University and the University of Washington (in Seattle), Santa Clara and Stanford, Fordham and Columbia, Fairfield and Yale, Boston College and Harvard, St. Joseph's (in

Philadelphia) and the University of Pennsylvania, Loyola of New Orleans and Tulane, Loyola in Maryland and Johns Hopkins. Similar pairings could be made for every one of the twenty-eight Jesuit colleges and universities in the United States. Invariably there is a neighboring institution that outweighs the Jesuit school in endowment, facilities, and prestige, even though the Jesuit institution compares quite favorably with these academic neighbors with respect to the quality and effectiveness of classroom teaching, openness to low-income students, and retention and graduation of minority students. This reflects the Jesuit idea of stewardship—carefully and creatively managing limited resources, working for a multiplier effect through a strong sense of commitment to students, and preparing first-generation college students for upward mobility and careers of competent and generous service to their communities. Forget for a moment the relative strength of financial endowments and physical plants. Just note the relative strength of Jesuit enterprises that are driven by generous human persons, lay and Jesuit, who are energized by a commitment to *cura personalis*, the personal care of students and others who are there to be served.[4]

Another comparison relates to the popular notion of talent and the twofold way in which Jesuits approach an understanding of that word. In the popular mind, there is a tendency to think of talented people simply as "gifted," effortlessly excelling at whatever they do. The popular mind overlooks the practice, the drill, the dedication, the development of that talent; the gift is mistaken for an achievement rather than the challenge and opportunity that it really is. In the Jesuit mind, there is gratitude for all gifts and talents and a serious sense of stewardship responsibility to use those gifts and talents well. Jesuit history is replete with stories of ordinary men developing their talents and using them extraordinarily well. Jesuit education takes students where they are and guides them along a path of development that is itself an exercise in excellence, in measured progress from a defined starting point.

All Jesuits are familiar with the parable of the talents (Matthew 25:14–30). A talent in biblical times was a monetary measure worth a substantial amount. In the parable, a man is about to embark on a journey. Before leaving, he distributes five talents to the first servant, two talents to the second, and one talent to the third. He doesn't give any particular instructions, although, as the story turns out, it is clear that he expects the servants to invest and manage the talents well. The first two servants are venturesome. Five talents become ten, and two become four. Upon his return, the master is quite pleased. The holder of the single talent, however, proves to be risk averse: "Master, I knew you were a demanding person, harvesting where you did not plant and gathering where you did not scatter; so out of fear I went off and buried your talent in the ground. Here it is back" (verses 24–25).

The master is not pleased. "You wicked, lazy servant! So you knew that I harvest where I did not plant and gather where I did not scatter? Should you not then have put my money in the bank so that I could have got it back with interest on my return? Now then! Take the talent from him and give it to the one with ten. . . . And throw this useless servant into the darkness outside" (verses 26–30).

Timidity has no place in the Jesuit way of life because timidity can convert a man of talent, great or small, into a "useless servant." The generous use of any talent the Lord wills to give him can make a man a faithful steward and a good Jesuit. Such a man is also free.

Deeds Not Words

The crowning meditation in the *Spiritual Exercises* is a summit reflection known as the "Contemplation to Attain the Love of God" (*SpEx*, 230). To be able to love God is a gift; this exercise helps dispose the retreatant to receive that gift and, in the process, learn something about the nature of love itself and of God, who is, as St. John states so simply, love (1 John 4:8). In every Jesuit life there must be a blending—a combination of the initiative called for in the parable of the talents and the sheer giftedness, the passive reception of the blessings that are recalled and reflected upon in the "Contemplation to Attain the Love of God." It is by reconciling these two forces—human initiative and divine generosity—that the Jesuit comes to terms with the use of wealth, power, and talent. This reconciliation is an exercise of Jesuit stewardship.

Ignatius presents two points that should be considered by the retreatant prior to making this exercise (known to Jesuits as the "Contemplatio"):

- The first is that love ought to manifest itself in deeds rather than in words.

- The second is that love consists in a mutual sharing of goods, for example, the lover gives and shares with the beloved what he possesses, or something of that which he has or is able to give; and vice versa, the beloved shares with the lover. Hence, if one has knowledge, he shares it with the one who does not possess it; and so also if one has honors, or riches. Thus, one always gives to the other. (*SpEx*, 230–31)

Ignatius invites the exercitant to place him- or herself in the presence of God, not in an imaginary exercise, but in a conscious realization that this is where every human stands—in the presence of God. Then Ignatius would have the exercitant ask for what he or she desires. "Here it will be to ask for an intimate knowledge of the many blessings received, that filled with gratitude for all, I may in all things love and serve the Divine Majesty" (*SpEx*, 233). All blessings are to be recalled to mind—creation, redemption, "and the special favors I have received" (*SpEx*, 234).

As an application of the prenote principle given above, Ignatius puts these thoughts in the mind of the retreatant: "I will ponder with great affection how much God our Lord has done [the deeds] for me, and how much He has given me [the sharing] of what He possesses, and finally, how much, as far as He can, the same Lord desires to give Himself to me according to His divine decrees" (*SpEx*, 234). Now the retreatant is ready to make the "Contemplatio."

In the first point of the meditation, Ignatius encourages the person at prayer to consider, "according to all reason and justice," what he or she should offer back to God. "Thus, as one would do who is moved by great feeling, I will make this offering of myself." And here you have the famous Jesuit prayer "Take and Receive," the "Suscipe," which is sung each year wherever Jesuits and lay colleagues gather at the altar for Mass on July 31, the Feast of St. Ignatius:

> Take, Lord, and receive all my liberty, my memory, my
>> understanding, and my entire will, all that I have
>> and possess.
> You have given it all to me. To you, Lord, I return it.
> All of it is yours;
> dispose of it wholly according to your will.
> Give me only your love and your grace,
> and that will be enough for me. Amen.

Moving on to the second point of his contemplation, Ignatius invites the person at prayer "to reflect how God dwells in creatures: in the elements giving them existence, in the plants giving them life, in the animals conferring upon them sensation, in man bestowing understanding. So He dwells in me and gives me being, life, sensation, intelligence; and makes a temple of me, since I am created in the likeness and image of the Divine Majesty" (*SpEx*, 235). It is easy to see how this reflection can go on for a long time; it is repeated several times in every full Ignatian retreat. And it is not difficult, once these thoughts are pondered, to see how Jesuits come by their characteristic outlook of "finding God in all things."

The third point of the "Contemplatio" promotes a considera-tion of "how God works and labors for me in all creatures upon the face of the earth, that is, He conducts Himself as one who labors. Thus, in the heavens, the elements, the plants, the fruits, the cattle, etc., He gives being, conserves them, confers life and sensation, etc. Then I will reflect on myself" (*SpEx*, 236).

In the fourth point, Ignatius considers "all blessings and gifts as descending from above. Thus, my limited power comes from the supreme and infinite power above, and so, too, my justice, good-ness, mercy, etc., descend from above as the rays of light descend from the sun, and as the waters flow from their fountains, etc." (*SpEx*, 237).

The Ignatian idea that love consists in a mutual sharing is the reconciling principle in Jesuit spirituality. Jesuits acknowledge every talent as a gift in need of development, and all wealth and power as stewardship responsibilities. They belong to God but are entrusted to our care for the service of others. That's the Jesuit outlook; that's the Jesuit way.

CHAPTER 11

The Standard of Christ

A phrase in the *Formula of the Institute of the Society of Jesus*, the document approved in 1540 by Pope Paul III that marked the formal establishment of the Society, has special meaning for all Jesuits. It might sound severe, off-putting, and not altogether ecumenical to persons not of our faith who like us and want to know us better. I repeat it here because without it we Jesuits cannot convey the essence of who we are. That phrase is *beneath the banner of the cross*.

> Whoever wishes to serve as a soldier of God beneath the banner of the cross in our Society, which we desire to be designated by the name of Jesus, and to serve the Lord alone and his vicar on earth, should keep in mind that once he has made a solemn vow of perpetual chastity he is a member of a community founded chiefly for this purpose: to strive especially for the progress of souls in Christian life and doctrine and for the propagation of the faith by the ministry of the word, by spiritual exercises and works of charity, and specifically by the education of children and unlettered persons in Christianity.[1]

The cross, the pope, the Word of God, the education of children and older persons who are unlettered in Christianity—these words and images might not leap immediately to mind when someone hears the word *Jesuit*. Nor does a picture of the "banner of the cross." But that is where we are, and that is where we want to be.

One of the key exercises in Ignatius's book of the Spiritual Exercises is the "Meditation on Two Standards." Each standard is symbolized by a banner or flag, something a military unit would call a *guidon*. But in reality the standards are competing value systems, ideologies, or mind-sets. One represents the values and strategy of Christ for the establishment of his kingdom; the other represents the opposing values and strategy of Satan.

Here are the exact words with which Ignatius sets the stage for this prayerful consideration (*SpEx*, 136–47):

A Meditation on Two Standards

The one of Christ, our supreme leader and lord, the other of Lucifer, the deadly enemy of our human nature.

Prayer. The usual preparatory prayer.

First Prelude. This is the history. Here it will be that Christ calls and wants all beneath His standard, and Lucifer, on the other hand, wants all under his.

Second Prelude. This is a mental representation of the place. It will be here to see a great plain, comprising the whole region about Jerusalem, where the sovereign Commander-in-Chief of all the good is Christ our Lord; and another plain about the region of Babylon, where the chief of the enemy is Lucifer.

Third Prelude. This is to ask for what I desire. Here it will be to ask for a knowledge of the deceits of the rebel chief and help to guard myself against them; and also to ask for a knowledge of the true life exemplified in the sovereign and true Commander, and the grace to imitate Him.

First Part: The Standard of Satan

First Point. Imagine you see the chief of all the enemy in the vast plain about Babylon, seated on a great throne of fire and smoke, his appearance inspiring horror and terror.

Second Point. Consider how he summons innumerable demons, and scatters them, some to one city and some to another, throughout the whole world, so that no province, no place, no state of life, no individual is overlooked.

Third Point. Consider the address he makes to them, how he goads them on to lay snares for men and bind them with chains. First they are to tempt them to covet riches (as Satan himself is accustomed to do in most cases) that they may the more easily attain the empty honors of this world, and then come to overweening pride.

The first step, then, will be riches, the second honor, the third pride. From these three steps the evil one leads to all other vices.

Second Part: The Standard of Christ

In a similar way, we are to picture to ourselves the sovereign and true Commander, Christ our Lord.

First Point. Consider Christ our Lord, standing in a lowly place in a great plain about the region of Jerusalem, His appearance beautiful and attractive.

Second Point. Consider how the Lord of all the world chooses so many persons, apostles, disciples, etc., and sends them throughout the whole world to spread His sacred doctrine among all men, no matter what their state or condition.

Third Point. Consider the address which Christ our Lord makes to all His servants and friends whom He sends on this enterprise, recommending to them to seek to help all, first by attracting them to the highest spiritual poverty, and should it please the Divine Majesty, and should He deign to choose them for it, even to actual poverty. Secondly, they should lead them to a desire for insults and contempt, for from these springs humility.

Hence, there will be three steps: the first, poverty as opposed to riches; the second, insults or contempt as opposed to the honor of this world; the third, humility as opposed to pride. From these three steps, let them lead men to all other virtues.

Colloquy. A colloquy should be addressed to our Lady, asking her to obtain for me from her Son and Lord the grace to be received under His standard, first in the highest spiritual poverty, and should the Divine Majesty be pleased thereby, and deign to choose and accept me, even in actual poverty; secondly, in bearing insults and wrongs, thereby to imitate Him better, provided only I can suffer these without sin on the part of another, and without offense of the Divine Majesty. Then I will say the *Hail Mary*.

Second Colloquy. This will be to ask her Son to obtain the same favors for me from the Father. Then I will say, *Soul of Christ*.

Third Colloquy. This will be to beg the Father to grant me the same graces. Then I will say the *Our Father*.

Ignatius saw the world as a battleground between the forces of good and the forces of evil, between Christ and Satan, the "enemy of our human nature." He saw the world as a place where men and women are called to act along with a God who is necessarily active in creation (otherwise creation would cease to exist). For Ignatius, Christ is, as Pedro de Leturia puts it, "the living and active King who has not yet completed the work entrusted to him by his Father. In order to bring that work to completion, he seeks, here and now, as in the past, generous collaborators and intimate friends whom he can send on such a mission."[2] The Jesuit is one who has responded to this invitation to be both collaborator and friend; the lines of the response are traced out for him in the "Meditation on Two Standards."

Centered on Christ

Jesuit spirituality is Christocentric; those who internalize it and adopt it cast their lot with Christ. His values are their values; his way is their way. They interpret all reality in and through the person of Jesus Christ.

The Christ upon whom any Jesuit's spirituality is centered is not only the attractive and engaging young man, thirty to thirty-three years of age, who was storyteller, healer, teacher, and celebrated preacher of the Sermon on the Mount. For a brief period in his life, Jesus carried a cross, was brutally beaten, humiliated, and killed. Even though this experience only lasted for a few days, it dominates the Christocentricity of Jesuit spirituality because it provides an interpretative framework within which one can discover the deeper meaning of human life; out of it all came glory. There was, after all, a resurrection victory and the establishment of a church in which Jesus now acts sacramentally, teaches through Scripture and tradition, and calls men and women to participate with him in the work he came to earth to do.

The Christocentricity of Jesuit spirituality rests on the *values* of Jesus (explained in his stories and teachings), the *example* of Jesus (visible in his lifestyle and choices—poverty, celibacy, obedience to the will of the Father), and the *determination* of Jesus to do battle with Satan and the forces of evil in order to win souls for the kingdom of God. The kingdom will one day "come," as we remind ourselves when repeating the Lord's Prayer, but it is incipient now on earth as a reign of justice and love. When the Jesuit prays, "Thy kingdom come," he thinks of his role, as a faithful follower of Christ, in lowering or removing the barriers—in human hearts and institutions—to the coming of the promised kingdom. His is a faith that wants to do justice.

The teller of the stories and teacher of the lessons that constitute the Sermon on the Mount (and other discourses recorded in the Gospels) stands at the center of Jesuit spirituality, as well as at the center of the plain Ignatius sketches in the meditative portrayal outlined above.

Ignatian imagination created a stylized center in the Exercises in the meditations on the kingdom of Christ and the two standards. The king who calls ("whoever wishes to join me in this enterprise must be willing to labor with me, that by following me in suffering, he may follow me in glory" [*SpEx*, 95]) and the bearer of the standard who proclaims a value system based on "poverty as opposed to riches; . . . insults or contempt as opposed to the honor of this world; [and] humility as opposed to pride" (*SpEx*, 146) are the same Jesus who proclaimed the good news articulated in the Sermon on the Mount. That great discourse, filled with principles for living the good life, begins with the Beatitudes and ends with this assertion: "Everyone who listens to these words of mine and acts on them will be like a wise man who built his house on rock. The rain fell, the floods came, and the winds blew and buffeted the house. But it did not collapse; it had been set solidly on rock. And everyone who listens to these words of mine but does not act on them will be like a fool who built his house on sand. The rain fell, the floods came, and the winds blew and buffeted the house. And it collapsed and was completely ruined" (Matthew 7:24–27).

Rock over Sand

The Jesuit chooses—as does anyone who follows Christ—rock over sand. The Jesuit's vows anchor him in a special way to Christ the rock; he also has, in the standard of Christ, a strategy that helps him avoid the quicksand of Satan's deceits. The personal goal of every Jesuit is to "persevere in running the race that lies before us while keeping our eyes fixed on Jesus, the leader and perfecter of faith. For the sake of the joy that lay before him he endured the cross, despising its shame, and has taken his seat at the right hand of the throne of God" (Hebrews 12:1–2).

Earlier on in the Exercises, Ignatius places the retreatant, who has emerged from a consideration of sin and personal sinfulness with a consciousness of being not only forgiven but also loved, before the crucified Christ. Conscious of himself or herself as a loved sinner, the retreatant asks in the presence of Christ crucified, "What have I done for Christ? What am I doing for Christ? What ought I to do for Christ?" And then Ignatius adds, for the retreatant's prayer, "As I behold Christ in this plight, nailed to the cross, I shall ponder upon what presents itself to my mind" (*SpEx*, 53).

There's been a lot of pondering on this point over the centuries. The content is unique to the person pondering. It is understandable, but regrettable, that the content of those personal ponderings—the high hopes, generous dreams, and apostolic ambitions—hidden deep in the heart of every Jesuit are not more transparent to those who see Jesuits doing their ordinary work every day. That's just the way we are.

Beyond the witness of our vows, I hope that there are some words and, more important, deeds of ours that effectively tell the world of our love of Christ. It becomes evident from time to time that we have a spiritual viewpoint that is shaped by the Exercises. For instance, when John Kenneth Galbraith's landmark book *The Affluent Society* was making the rounds in the late 1950s, the author's comments about the "basic benefits" of wealth struck me as a frighteningly familiar echo of the standard of Satan. Here is what Galbraith wrote: "Broadly speaking, there are three basic benefits from wealth. First is the satisfaction in the power with which it endows the individual. Second is the physical possession of the things which money can buy. Third is the distinction or esteem that accrues to the rich man as a result of his wealth."[3]

The power-possession-esteem triad echoes the strategy Ignatius saw as the trap set by the enemy of our human nature. Jesuit antennae are attuned to these cultural currents. One of my Jesuit friends likes to suggest to students, who are barraged daily by televised or print ads that are the infrastructure of our culture of consumerism, that they should say, "Ask not what this ad invites you to buy; ask what this ad expects you to be!" All too often the only honest answer is, "A materialistic, hedonistic, personally insecure consumer, who might also be a sex maniac given the sex appeal that underlies so many sales pitches." Ignatius was not explicit about sex when he outlined the elements of the standard of Satan. He simply observed, after mentioning riches, honor, and pride, that "from these three steps the evil one leads to all other vices" (*SpEx*, 142).

Knowing Where the Traps Are

Jesuit spirituality is surely at home with the world; in fact, Jesuits are often both admired and criticized for being worldly. The reason they can carry it off without losing either integrity or fidelity to their charism is their rootedness in the standard of Christ. They know where the traps are. They are also well aware that there is a triple concupiscence in every human heart—male, female, Jesuit, lay, rich, poor—and that a famous passage in the first letter of John can serve as a helpful commentary on the Ignatian meditation on the standards:

> Do not love the world or the things of the world. If anyone loves the world, the love of the Father is not in him. For all that is in the world, sensual lust, enticement for the eyes, and a pretentious life, is not from the Father but is from the world. Yet the world and its enticement are passing away. But whoever does the will of God remains forever. (2:15–17)

Correctly understood, "the world," in John's view, means opposition to God, forces hostile to God. It is not that the world is evil in any sense; it is simply, as John saw it, estranged, unredeemed, and in need of salvation. "For God so loved the world," says the Gospel of John, "that he gave his only Son, so that everyone who believes in him might not perish but might have eternal life. For God did not send his Son into the world to condemn the world, but that the world might be saved through him" (3:16–17). The world is good; make no mistake about that.

There is nothing wrong with being immersed in the things of the world. Anyone who wants to be appropriately worldly, indeed anyone who wants to work with Christ for the salvation of the world, simply has to deal first with those energies or drives from within that could ruin otherwise good intentions. John highlights three lusts that are familiar to us all: the lust of the flesh, the lust to possess what attracts the eye, and the lust for power over others. These are natural human drives for sexual union, possession of material things, and pride-producing prestige. Management of these drives, according to God's will for him, is made easier for the Jesuit by his commitment to the strategy outlined in the standard of Christ. That's why he chooses to serve "beneath the banner of the cross."

Jesuits, although Christocentric in their vocational commitment and outlook, are characteristically appreciative and respectful of the non-Christian faith commitments of others. There is a welcome mat out for persons of other faiths at the entrance to Jesuit educational institutions and retreat houses, as well as any other place where Jesuits assemble to serve. Though sometimes accused of bending over backward to avoid offending persons of other faiths, and muting, hiding, or watering down the explicitly Catholic identity of their lives and works, Jesuits do need occasional reassurance that the non-Catholic, non-Christian associates in their various enterprises expect them to display their Catholic, Christian, Ignatian colors—modestly and discreetly, perhaps, but always without apology.

Countless times over the years I've been asked to give an invocation or benediction at some public function. More often than not, I do not conclude the public prayer, which is being offered in the name of the entire assembly, with the words *through Christ our Lord*, words that are so familiar and completely appropriate in Catholic settings. As one praying with, for, and in the name of a religiously diverse group, I take care not to exclude anyone from the opportunity to add a personal amen to the public prayer. Even persons of no faith at all want to be part of that moment. Although no one would seriously suggest that a public prayer should be addressed "to whom it may concern," most people appreciate sensitivity to religious differences in prayerful public moments.

Ignatius often referred to God as our "Creator and Lord." Jesuits pray to that same God in public and private, hope to lead others to that God by word, work, and example, and reserve a place of honor for that God in all their institutions, which, after all, are there for the greater glory of that same God.

On Speaking Ignatian

Father George W. Traub, SJ, director of Ignatian programs at Xavier University in Cincinnati, published a small booklet under the title *Do You Speak Ignatian? A Glossary of Terms Used in Ignatian and Jesuit Circles*. Lay colleagues and other friends will appreciate his explanation of the letters *IHS*, seen everywhere in Jesuit circles: "The first three letters, in Greek, of the name *Jesus*. These letters appear as a symbol on the official seal of the Society of Jesus or Jesuits." I would add that they appear today all over the world as signs of Jesuit life and culture; they mark the centrality of Jesus Christ to everything that Jesuits do.

Similarly helpful is Father Traub's entry after the name *Jesuit*:

> Noun. A member of the Society of Jesus. The term was originally coined as a putdown by people who felt there was something terribly arrogant about a group calling itself the Company or Society of Jesus, whereas previous religious orders had been content to name themselves after their founder (e.g., "Benedictines," "Franciscans," "Dominicans"). Later the title was adopted as a shorthand

name by members of the Society themselves, as well as by others favorable to them.

Adjective. Pertaining to the Society of Jesus. The negative term, now that *Jesuit* has been rehabilitated, is *Jesuitical* meaning "sly" or "devious."

There is nothing sly or devious about Father Traub's entry under *God*. I reproduce it here because it will help you better understand the mind of Ignatius and thus the mind of every Jesuit:

> Various titles or names are given to the Mystery underlying all that exists—e.g., the Divine, Supreme Being, the Absolute, the Transcendent, the All-Holy—but all of these are only "pointers" to a Reality beyond human naming and beyond our limited human comprehension. Still, some conceptions are taken to be less inadequate than others within a given tradition founded in revelation. Thus Jews reverence *Yahweh* (a name so holy it is better not spoken, but rather an alternative name is used), and Muslims worship *Allah* (the [only] God).
>
> Christians conceive of the one God as "Trinity," as having three "ways of being"—(1) Creator and covenant partner (from Hebrew tradition) or "Father" (the "Abba" of Jesus' experience), (2) "Son" incarnate (become human) in Jesus, and (3) present everywhere in the world through the "Spirit."

Ignatius of Loyola had a strong Trinitarian sense of God, but he was especially fond of the expression *the Divine Majesty*, which stresses the greatness, or "godness," of God. The twentieth-century Jesuit theologian Karl Rahner talked of "the incomprehensible Mystery of self-giving Love."

That mystery is revealed, if not fully explicated, in the life, death, resurrection, and ascension of Jesus Christ, in whose life and under whose cross Jesuits search for meaning in their attempts to live their own personal lives of self-giving love.

CHAPTER 12

The Harvest Is Ready

Most Jesuits think a lot about vocations to the Society—the mystery of their own and the extent to which young men are now being called and choosing to respond to that call.

All of us know that it really is a call, not a choice, although we have to choose, by God's grace, to respond to the call. It is God's work to call men to and sustain them in the Society, but we also acknowledge that it is up to us to do a few things on the human side that will improve the acoustics for those being called and increase the level of encouragement they need if they are to offer a positive response. The power to attract men to the Jesuit life is clearly and exclusively with the Lord; some essential tasks, however, are our responsibility. Fatalism in the face of the present decline in the number of vocations would be an unworthy and surely ineffective response to this strategic question: What can we do, in addition to prayer, to foster an increase in vocations to the Society?

There is a good deal of research on factors that influence a personal decision to become a priest or religious.[1] Psychological, sociological, and anthropological analysis is available to ground theological reflection on this issue. Most of the research focuses on vocations to diocesan priesthood, but much is applicable to the decision to become a Jesuit.

Research findings and my own personal observations prompt me to put some thoughts about the vocation issue here at the end of this book. I hope other Jesuits, along with lay friends who care about our future, will give serious thought to this issue so that we can develop, compare, and test some strategies at local, provincial, or national levels. We Jesuits do not exactly fit into the picture Peter Maurin used to paint for Dorothy Day with his characteristic wit: "The trouble with the world is that the people who do all the acting never think and the people who do all the thinking never act."[2] But we can run the risk of misdirected activity by recruiters or ponderous passivity on the part of other Jesuits who are not charged with recruitment responsibilities. All of us should be doing more, but what is it that we should be doing?

Thinking Strategically about Vocations

I'd like to apply a since/therefore approach to the task of compiling a list of some strategic steps that might be directed to the vocation challenge. In what follows, the "since" clause will express a principle or presupposition; the "therefore," or follow-up, clause will introduce a strategic step that might be taken by us.

Since there has never been a Jesuit who has not been born of a woman, and since many women now feel alienated from and consider themselves unappreciated by the Church, it would, therefore, seem wise for us to work with women (mothers of students as well as female students, retreatants, and parishioners), learning what they think about the Jesuit vocation and inviting them to help us, if they can, by encouraging their sons or male friends to become Jesuits.

Since celibacy is an organizing principle for our life together in community, and since only men called to celibacy can be called to the Society, it would, therefore, make sense to help young men by discerning with them the presence or absence of a call to celibacy before focusing on a possible call to priesthood or brotherhood in the Society. The appeal of the apostolate is not to be reduced to small print, of course; my point is simply that celibacy is a central consideration.

Since a vocation to the Society is a sacred calling to a uniquely spiritual role, it would, therefore, be strategically important not only to open the Ignatian treasure of the Spiritual Exercises to potential candidates but also to invite them to develop their spirituality in our Christian Life Communities, the successor organization to the Sodalities that fostered so many Jesuit vocations a generation or two ago.

Since all research reports highlight the importance of "being asked" in the minds of those who eventually followed the call, it is, therefore, crucially important to encourage every Jesuit to invite promising young men to consider our way of life.

Since we are contemplatives in action, we should, therefore, want to offer young men the assurance that meaningful apostolic work (action) awaits them in the Society. It is up to us to present to the young the spectacle of ourselves as happy men doing useful work; it is also up to us to offer them the prospect of having challenging work to do that they could not do if they were not Jesuits, or at least could not do in the Jesuit way if they were not Jesuits. And in keeping with our charism as contemplatives in action, care should be taken to point out the spiritual, or contemplative, dimension of all our works.

Since the candidates we want to attract are not looking for an easy life, and since Ignatius would not have us forget that poverty is "the firm wall of religion," we should, therefore, take care to live simply and avoid projecting an image of affluence. If what we have by way of food, drink, housing, hardware, software, wheels, and other equipment is not recognizable to young observers as part of a necessary tool kit for the apostolate, they will be puzzled, confused, probably critical, and inclined to keep on looking.

Since Hispanics are fast becoming the dominant ethnic group in the U.S. Catholic community, we should, therefore, be able to "go in their door"—easily and comfortably—in our search for candidates. If fluency in Spanish were more widespread among North American Jesuits, and if every non-Hispanic candidate knew he would be expected to master spoken and written Spanish before taking vows, the challenge of it all might have some appeal.

Since some kind of visual identification with the group reinforces one's sense of belonging and pride of membership in the group, it would, therefore, seem wise to employ the seal of the Society (on a lapel shield or button) as a universal symbol of membership in an apostolic band of brothers that dates back to 1540. Some external sign will allow prospective candidates to "see" us more easily and to imagine themselves as one of us. The emblem identifies the wearer as "one" among an important and significant "many," understood by insiders as "this least Society" in the eyes of God.

Since provision of an opportunity to serve on a foreign mission sets the Society of Jesus apart from diocesan seminaries in the minds of young men in the U.S., we should, therefore, be sure to point out the links a given province has with identifiable overseas ministries.

Since research identifies those of an age to be considering the Society as hesitant about making permanent commitments, yet yearning for meaning in their lives, we should, therefore, point to our privilege of taking perpetual vows within two years and our tradition of obedience as potential solutions to their search for meaning. The young reflect a cultural bias toward "keeping all options open" and preserving "freedom to choose." We can offer commitment-with-flexibility in the variety of apostolates available worldwide to any willing Jesuit. We should let them know that a Jesuit must declare himself to be willing to work anywhere in the world. We also have our uniquely Jesuit charism of availability in obedience to the Holy See with respect to any mission the Holy Father invites us to undertake.

Since our tradition favors a formation characterized by intellectual rigor, and since our work in the intellectual apostolate has, at the invitation of papal leadership, strengthened the Church over the centuries, we should, therefore, be careful not to relax standards and not to abandon intellectual apostolates in favor of other good works that other religious and diocesan priests do routinely and well. What sets us apart is our ability to blend thought and action, analysis and service, scholarship and pastoral concern. Letting these linkages become more visible to young men of talent may well serve to attract them to our Company.

These points for strategic thinking are intended to open up comment and reflection on this topic. Affluence in the U.S. and materialism in the broader culture explain to some extent the reduced interest in vocations to the Society. But out of that same materialistic culture many candidates are presenting themselves for ordained ministry in other denominations, and diocesan seminaries seem to be doing better than religious orders in attracting young Catholic men. Why are not more candidates coming to us?

The sexual revolution that began in the 1960s means that there is less ignorance and innocence in sexual matters now. The sexual histories of those who entered the Society in the '40s and '50s were significantly different from the histories interested candidates might present today. "During the Sexual Revolution," quips newspaper columnist and television commentator Mark Shields, "I was a conscientious objector." There are fewer today who were conscientious objectors in their high school and college years, and this helps explain the rise of celibacy as a barrier-to-entry in the minds of many young men when they consider our way of life. Ignatius's personal history as well as Ignatian spirituality can speak persuasively to sensitive and generous young men who want to disengage themselves from a concupiscent culture long enough to face up to the question of a call to follow Christ in the Society.

As I acknowledged at the outset, it is God's work to call men to the Society, but this doesn't mean that there is nothing to be done by us. We cannot remain passive, and we certainly don't want to stop thinking about the problem. We cannot control social forces or prevent cultural shifts, but we can adapt to them. Our immediate task is to figure out what might be best to do in the midst of all our limitations and then just go ahead, trusting in the Lord, and do it.

From the points I've outlined above, I would cull this set of strategic steps that any province in the U.S., or all the North American provinces together, might consider: (1) work with women; (2) focus on celibacy; (3) multiply our Christian Life Communities; (4) overcome our hesitation to ask; (5) describe our works and, where the principle of assignment is unavailable to us (in other words, where a provincial cannot simply assign a man to a job in an institution), negotiate with those who control hiring in our Jesuit institutions reliable means whereby qualified Jesuits can be offered jobs; (6) run a lifestyle check in local communities; (7) open up to Hispanic culture and target Hispanics as potential candidates; (8) adopt a modest emblem, a sign of membership to be worn by Jesuits; (9) emphasize our ties to opportunities for foreign service; (10) present vowed commitment and Jesuit obedience as answers in the search for meaning; (11) let it be known that we still place a premium on the intellect.

That last point may not be as easy to "sell" these days as it once was. In the broader American society some young people are turning away from science because of what they perceive to be the misuses of science in their day. In the Society of Jesus (and in the minds of those considering becoming Jesuits) some are turning away from the intellectual apostolate because of a perceived irrelevance of that work to the pressing needs of the poor and oppressed. Obviously there is a need for interpretation and persuasion on both fronts. We need the help of our lay colleagues in analyzing the problem and in making a convincing case for vocations to the Society.

Sociological Surroundings

With all of this said, and with a clear acknowledgment and reaffirmation of the fact that it is all God's work, this business of calling men to priesthood, I want to reflect further on what I like to think of as the sociological surroundings of priesthood in our part of the world today.

When I was a high school boy at St. Joseph's Prep in Philadelphia, our priest-principal, Father John F. Lenny ("Big John," as we all called this tall, gruff, but cultured Jesuit whose five o'clock shadow began to appear around ten in the morning), told a school assembly that a vocation to the priesthood was given by God in response to the virtuous life of the recipient's mother. It didn't occur to me then that his analysis was putting a bit of unfair freight on the shoulders of a youngster who had no interest in the priesthood but nonetheless thought that his mother was perfect! In later years, however, I did think that there might be some scriptural basis for that position as I reflected on the first chapter of 1 Samuel, where Hannah vows to the Lord, "If you look with pity on the misery of your handmaid, if you remember me and do not forget me, if you give your handmaid a male child, I will give him to the LORD for as long as he lives" (verse 11). And, as we know from the biblical account, "the LORD remembered her" and granted her request (verse 19). She "bore a son whom she called Samuel, since she had asked the LORD for him" (verse 20).

There are obviously more mothers and surely no less virtue now. But there is also less urgent prayer and desire today on the part of mothers to give their children to the service of the Lord, at least insofar as that service would be specified by priesthood and religious life.

My prep school principal's theology of priestly vocation could be faulted for ignoring the role of the virtuous father, if indeed parental virtue can be considered a significant factor in any case. Even so, fathers are not storming heaven these days with prayers that their sons might be called to the priesthood.

Among the personal effects left behind by Father John W. Tynan, SJ, after his death in 1960 was a letter from his father, received shortly after young Jack Tynan left his home in Jersey City to enter the Jesuit novitiate in 1919. His dad, expressing a faith that echoed Hannah's, wrote to his son:

> You gave me one of the greatest joys of my life when you told
> me you had joined the Jesuits. I never mentioned a vocation
> to you because I believe the Almighty reserves calling men
> to the priesthood to Himself. Years before the Holy Hour
> was begun in St. Bridget's, I used to have one on my own
> on Saturday nights. I never could meditate, so I prayed and
> hoped and begged and cried, yes, and sometimes I fell asleep,
> all in one hour. You were often the subject of my thoughts.
> I said many a time to our blessed Lord, "I'll waive the plea-
> sure of ever seeing his back at the altar as a priest, only call
> him—for Kalamazoo, or Hong Kong, or Jersey City."

Shortly after writing that letter, Mr. Tynan died. And with him
went an era characterized not only by the "Holy Hour" and the
"back at the altar" but also by tears and prayers focused on the call
to priesthood for one's son. It would be rare today to hear a father
describe his reaction to a son's decision to enter the seminary as
"one of the greatest joys of my life."

Why don't fathers pray today as Jack Tynan's father did? Where is
the Church that fostered such prayer? Fathers still pray, of course,
and the institutional Church is still very much present in our midst,
but the sociological surroundings are markedly different. They are
splitting at three prominent seams: (1) several decades of seeing
men leave the priesthood (raising the question, Why?), (2) debate
about the desirability of having a married Roman Catholic clergy
(suggesting the question, Why not?), and (3) plenty of talk about
the possibility of women priests in the Catholic Church (keeping alive the question of whether this is something that would be
clearly impossible for an all-powerful God to bring about).

A fourth consideration, surely worthy of mention and probably
still discouraging and diverting interest in priesthood on the part
of potential candidates and their parents, is the news that broke
in 2002 that a small but not insignificant percentage of priests,
including Jesuits, had sexually abused minors. The whole sexual
abuse scandal rocked the American Church as nothing had ever

before, and the Church has not yet worked its way through this crisis.

There were failures in dioceses and religious orders to screen potential candidates carefully and, worse, later to advance some to ordination who should never have been ordained. Moreover, the mismanagement of so many "cases" that did come to the attention of superiors damaged public confidence in the integrity and competence of those in charge. Who wants to join an organization like that? Who wants to be associated with men who do such terrible things? The immediate answer for many is: No one. Further reflection, however, sees God still there, still calling, and the seminaries as centers of solid spirituality and houses of sound formation. But a new prejudice is now in place and it is taking a toll that is part of the very heavy price the Church is paying for the sins of its past.

Long before the scandal broke, Jesuit psychiatrist James J. Gill looked into cases of one hundred men who left the priesthood in the late 1960s (not all of them Jesuits, by any means) and identified *depression* as the common denominator characterizing most of these departures. Typically, the priests studied were task-oriented men, somewhat compulsive and perfectionistic about their work, and possessed of unconscious drives for recognition and approval from superiors and those they served in their various ministries. Since childhood they successfully met performance goals in fidelity to household chores, newspaper delivery routes, early morning Mass-serving schedules, athletic excellence, and academic honors. With each achievement came approval and satisfaction. The individual came to perceive his own value as deriving from *doing* things rather than from simply *being* a person. Ridiculous as it sounds when you say it out loud, these men thought of themselves as human doings, not human beings. It is not so ridiculous, however, when you note that this doing-over-being perspective is characteristic of an accepted value reversal in the broader secular culture in which these men live and work.

The seminary track provided the men Father Gill studied with still more difficult goals and achievements, thus deepening the unconscious drive for recognition and approval. The pattern extended on through ordination and priestly ministry. During and after the Second Vatican Council, however, we began to notice in the Church not only an emerging laity but also a declining esteem for the status of priesthood in the popular imagination, as well as in the mind of the priest himself. Approval stopped coming automatically or easily from the pews; when it came, it was less regular and less enthusiastic. The unconscious appetite for recognition was not being satisfied. Here is how Father Gill explained what was going on:

> After a number of years in the ministry (usually between five and fifteen) they feel their parishioners are taking them for granted. Nobody seems to care how hard they work to prepare a sermon or teach a class. They have so consistently performed in a better-than-average and reliable manner that their bishops and religious superiors simply expect them to do a good job. Applause comes less frequently as the years go by. They begin to feel more and more dissatisfied with themselves, with their role in the Church, and with the requirements of celibacy. At the point where the man becomes unhappy with his lot in life and pessimistic about his future, some sensitive woman accurately perceives his deep need for someone to love him—not for his performance or accomplishments but just for his own sake. He responds with gratitude and love. She has brought a kind of joy into his life which has been absent until now. She has lifted him at least part way out of his state of depression, and he feels he can't afford to lose her. He decides to marry and leave the priesthood.[3]

Although decades old, this explanation still remains useful in understanding the human side of the institution of priesthood. It does not, however, explain satisfactorily why fewer young men are considering the priesthood today.

The New Catholic World

A man who entered seminary before and during the Second Vatican Council came out of a world that no longer exists and offered himself for service in a Church that no longer exists. In the old days, priesthood was a "step up" socially in the Catholic community; that's no longer the case. The old Catholic culture saw priests as necessary for saving souls and viewed Catholic schools as fortresses of the faith that simply had to be staffed. All the "faithful" paid up generously—the laity with their money and the gift of sons or daughters, priests and religious with their lives. The motivation for the generosity and the sacrifice related to "saving my own soul and the souls of others" was tinged with fear. Today there is less anxiety about saving "my" soul or the souls of others, not because the actual barriers to eternal life have been lowered, and not through any disinterest in salvation, but for several other reasons. Presumption may be on the rise, but whatever the cause, there is a lot less fear of going to hell these days. Why let avoidance of that possibility dominate vocational decision making?

Ministry is still necessary for salvation, but not necessarily ordained ministry—or so the young seem to be thinking. It is more difficult now to make the case for the need for ordained ministers. There is still a harvest to be brought in, but the multiplication of lay ministries may be distracting the young from paying much attention to the appropriate number of priests needed to serve the worldwide Church adequately in the immediate future.

Fear is, in any case, a less powerful motivator today in the personal resolution of the religious or priestly vocation issue in the minds of the young. Anxieties (occasionally planted in parochial school classrooms of the old Church and exploited in those days by vocation recruiters) about losing one's soul for failure to respond to the call are hardly operative in today's Church, which finds itself on much better terms with the world.

Fear of their own sexuality was widespread among immigrant young people, especially the Irish portion of the Church in the first half of the twentieth century. That fear was reinforced by the preaching of the clergy and the moral instruction in Catholic schools. Some of the young saw in celibacy a built-in, prepackaged, lifelong resolution of that fear. As the Catholic environment ceased being supportive of those exaggerated fears and as both preaching and instruction gave greater recognition to the beauty and value of sexuality, the young became more comfortable with their humanity. Many of those who had bought into celibacy decades earlier as a kind of life-insurance policy and who were lugging it through life as so much baggage began to see for the first time not only that there was an alternative (they knew that all along) but also that the alternative was something true, good, and beautiful. Moreover, the sociological surroundings exhibited signs of acceptance and encouragement for those who wanted to change their lives and leave the priesthood or religious life.

Another change in the American Catholic community related to economic status. We were a poor people, we Catholics, in the first few generations of our life as the immigrant Church in America. When the number of candidates for seminaries and novitiate began to drop in the 1960s, an elderly Christian brother, who was a veteran vocation promoter, remarked to me, "There just aren't enough lean, hungry boys around anymore!" It is probably true that on a natural plane some interest in vocations was generated by the absence of job opportunities during the Great Depression. It is certainly true that the spread of affluence in the American Catholic community and our concomitant addiction to comfort have dampened the spirit of self-sacrifice that many believe to be the soil in which the call to ordained or consecrated ministry takes root. It is significant, I think, that a young college graduate who entered a Jesuit novitiate about a decade *after* we began thinking of America as the "affluent society" had on the wall of his room a hand-lettered quotation from Carl Sandburg: "Tell them too much money has killed men and left them dead years before burial."

If you were to take a look through a socioeconomic window at the occupations pursued by many of the fathers of those who entered seminaries and novitiates before the 1960s, you would see a lot of blue-collar workers with modest incomes and even more modest educational attainments. Many of those jobs are now automated out of existence or held by persons who have no strong ties to the Catholic Church community.

To the extent that the Spartan simplicities imposed by modest economic circumstances might have freed a young person to respond to a call to the priesthood, a source of vocations has largely dried up in the American Church. Curiously and paradoxically, we are doing so well economically that we may have priced ourselves out of the vocation market.

Similar measures could be taken to examine the distance (social, economic, and even psychological) between the old urban Catholic neighborhoods with their relationship to parish life, and the suburbs and exurbs where so many Catholic families now live. Comparative indicators of family incomes, real assets, educational attainment, and club memberships would reveal socioeconomic progress that has moved the Catholic family quite literally into another world. Striking changes are also apparent in rural communities.

The institutional Church and its parochial bases appear to exercise a far less significant pull on the loyalties and vocational commitments of the affluent young, so many of whom are growing up far away from the old neighborhoods where the Catholic parish of their parents and grandparents is, all too often, dead or dying. In those once Catholic inner-city neighborhoods, however, there are now Asian, Hispanic, and African American youth, not all by any means Catholic, and those who are Catholic are not untouched by the cultural influences that mar the acoustics for a call to the priesthood.

I grew up in a Philadelphia neighborhood known as East Germantown. My nephews and nieces and their entire generation grew up in a neighborhood called Television, where just about all their neighbors are young, rich, stylishly dressed, and good-looking. The eyes of the young, both rich and poor, are bigger than their budget, thanks to television. Travel is their substitute for commitment, now that television has opened up for them a window on the world. They live their lives in the middle of an expectations explosion. As a result, the well-educated and well-off have little time and precious little inclination to listen for a call to sell all they have (or might acquire) and give it to the poor, say no to marriage, and make a permanent commitment to follow a celibate Christ.

Is Affluenza the Enemy?

The richer Americans get, the more we seem to want and the more restless (less satisfied) we become. Writing in the *Baltimore Sun* about our national "level of prosperity that previous generations could not have imagined," Marilyn Geewax warned, "Unless we can find a cure for our affluenza, we may end up with very full landfills and very empty lives in our older years." The Jesuit vocation has a way of filling up what otherwise might have been an empty life.

I believe, along with Jack Tynan's father, that "the Almighty reserves calling men to the priesthood to Himself." It is possible that fewer are being called today because fewer are needed for the *old* forms of ministry. To the extent that we Jesuits move creatively and effectively into new forms of ministry (which would include doing old ministries in a new way) and to the extent that we rediscover our roots and renew both our ministries and ourselves in the traditional apostolates, including the educational apostolates, I think we will attract the faith-committed young whose high-hearted love of Christ will have plenty of room to grow in our Company.

We are looking for fully human beings with well-integrated personalities who are capable of being agents of change in a world of uncertainty. I'm sure we Jesuits will keep thinking and praying a lot about vocations. I hope many young men will continue to think and pray about the possibility of a vocation with us. It is possible to find the answers to life's questions in the Jesuit vocation; it is a sure thing that you will find meaningful work and great companionship in addition to growth in a faith community.

If this looks to you like a vocation advertisement, see what you can do to bring it to the attention of someone who might be searching for what we have to offer. The "harvest is ready," and we need more good men to help us gather it in.

There will always be Saturdays until the end of time. Time is measured in seconds, minutes, hours, days, weeks, months, and years, and one of those days in every week will always be a Saturday. Whether or not there will be *Jesuit* Saturdays until the end of time is another story. Mine are surely numbered, I know; exactly how many more Saturdays will have a place in the history of the Society of Jesus is known to God alone. I certainly hope the Jesuit order will be "helping souls" until the end of time. But who can say?

Young men can say yes at any time to a Jesuit vocation, and if they do, the order will continue. They can also say no. Moreover, it is possible that sometime in the future there will be no one saying yes or no because God, in his infinite wisdom, will have stopped calling candidates to follow Christ in the Jesuit way. That is possible. If it happens, other ways will still be there, and new ways will open up. The Church will continue. Jesus promised to be with the Church, not with any particular religious community, until the end of time (Matthew 28:20).

My prayer is that the Society of Jesus will live forever. And I make that prayer in the spirit of Jeremiah 17:7: "Blessed is the man who trusts in the LORD, / whose hope is the Lord."

I hope, Lord, that you will maintain "this least Society" for your service and glory; you are my hope. All I can do is trust in you, Lord, to make it happen.

Epilogue

As this revised edition goes to press, the Thirty-Fifth General Congregation of the Society of Jesus has just concluded its work in Rome. We have a new superior general—seventy-one-year-old, Spanish-born Adolfo Nicolas. Elected on the second ballot on January 19, 2008, Father Nicolas later met the press and, among other things, said: "My current attitude is to listen, listen and obey. As you know, the General Congregation has authority over Father General. During the General Congregation I am subject to the Congregation. If the Congregation tells me what needs to be done, what direction to take in the future, I should obey, that is my mission. Therefore, what is important to me now is to know what the General Congregation wishes; as well as how to respond to the challenges that the Holy Father has sent us."

First, I'll offer a word about the challenges presented by the Holy Father and then give a summary of what the Congregation discussed.

Pope Benedict XVI welcomed Father Nicolas in a private audience and encouraged him to continue the "dialogue with culture" that began for the new general thirty-three years earlier when he began working in Japan. The Pope also urged the new Jesuit leader to ensure a "thorough formation" for young Jesuits. Father Nicolas reaffirmed his personal respect for the Vicar of Christ and conveyed to Pope Benedict the desire of the whole Society to serve the Church all over the world.

On February 21, 2008, as the Congregation was drawing to a close, all the delegates together with their new general went to the Vatican for an audience with the Holy Father. In his opening remarks to the Pope, Father Nicolas explained, "What inspires and impels us [Jesuits] is the Gospel and the Spirit of Christ. If the Lord Jesus was not at the center of our life we would have no sense of our apostolic activity, we would have no reason for our existence. It is from the Lord Jesus we learn to be near to the poor and suffering, to those who are excluded in this world."

Here are highlights of the Pope's message that day to the Society as summarized later in a memorandum issued by the Congregation:

> The service of faith and the promotion of justice must be kept united. Pope Benedict reminded us that the injustice that breeds poverty has "structural causes," which must be fought, and that the source of this commitment can be found in the faith itself: "the preferential option for the poor is implicit in the Christological faith in the God who became poor for us, so as to enrich us with his poverty (cf. 2 Cor 8.9)." By sending us to "those physical and spiritual places which others do not reach or have difficulty in reaching," the Pope entrusts to us the task to "build bridges of understanding and dialogue," according to the best tradition of the Society, in the diversity of its ministries: the Society of Jesus has lived extraordinary experiences of proclamation and encounter between the Gospel and world cultures—it suffices to think of Matteo Ricci in China, Roberto De Nobili in India or of the "Reductions" in Latin America. And you are rightly proud of them. I feel it is my duty today to urge you to set out once again in the tracks of your predecessors with the same courage and intelligence, but also with an equally profound motivation of faith and enthusiasm to serve the Lord and his Church.

The Congregation itself issued separate decrees on Jesuit identity, mission, collaboration (understood as "apostolic companionship based on discernment and oriented toward service") with laity and others, obedience, and governance. As Father Nicolas indicated, the Congregation is his superior; these decrees, even though broad ranging, are his marching orders. The implementation process has now begun.

As was the case with decrees from past Congregations, these will be discussed and implemented worldwide. There will be some changes in governance structures and the geographic configuration of provinces, but the Ignatian essentials remain the same and the Society will, in the words of Peter Lippert, continue "to live on the trust that it places in its individual members."

The question remains, however, as to how successful we will be, with God's grace, in attracting new members. Who will be there in Jesuit boots, shoes, or sandals, to, as Pope Benedict put it, "set out in the tracks" of earlier Jesuits "with the same courage and intelligence" and with their "faith and enthusiasm to serve the Lord and his Church."?

To say that there may well be fewer Jesuits in the twenty-first century than there were in the twentieth is not to say that there will be none. My hope-based prayer is that the Ignatian spirit will be alive and well for centuries to come in our world. I also pray that the bearers of that spirit will be both Jesuit and lay, in numbers that match up exactly with the mysterious but not altogether unknowable will of God.

ENDNOTES

Introduction

1. William J. Byron, SJ, *Quadrangle Considerations* (Chicago: Loyola University Press, 1989); William J. Byron, SJ, *Take Your Diploma and Run: Speaking to the Next Generation* (New York: Paulist Press, 1992).

Chapter 1: The Man Who Was Loyola

1. Pedro de Ribandeneira, *Vita Patris Ignatii*, lib. I, c. ii, in *Fontes narrativi de S. Ignatio de Loyola et de Societatis Jesu initiis*, ed. D. Fernández Zapico, Candido de Dalmases, and Pedro de Leturia, 4 vols. (Rome, 1943–60), 4:85, quoted in Candido de Dalmases, SJ, *Ignatius of Loyola: Founder of the Jesuits* (St. Louis: Institute of Jesuit Sources, 1985), p. 32.
2. John C. Olin, ed., *The Autobiography of St. Ignatius Loyola* (New York: Harper Torchbooks, 1974), p. 22.
3. Dalmases, *Ignatius of Loyola*, p. 53.
4. Quotations from the *Spiritual Exercises* are cited in the text with the abbreviation listed below. The number following the abbreviation refers to the section where the quotation can be found. In some cases, quotations have been changed to reflect gender-inclusive language.
   SpEx: Louis J. Puhl, SJ, trans., *The Spiritual Exercises of St. Ignatius of Loyola: A New Translation* (Westminster, Md.: Newman Press, 1951).
5. This prayer, attributed to St. Ignatius, reflects but does not repeat verbatim words from the *Spiritual Exercises*. It can be found in Michael Harter, SJ, ed., *Hearts on Fire: Praying with Jesuits* (St. Louis: Institute of Jesuit Sources, 1993), p. 35.
6. H. O. Evennett, *The Spirit of the Counter-Reformation*, ed. John Bossy (Cambridge: Cambridge University Press, 1968), p. 45, quoted in Olin, *Autobiography of St. Ignatius Loyola*, p. 12.

Chapter 2: Why We Are in Higher Education

1. Quotations from the Complementary Norms are cited in the text with the abbreviation listed below. The number following the abbreviation refers to the section where the quotation can be found.

    CN: *The Constitutions of the Society of Jesus and Their Complementary Norms: A Complete English Translation of the Official Latin Texts* (St. Louis: Institute of Jesuit Sources, 1996).

2. William J. Byron, SJ, *Answers from Within: Spiritual Guidelines for Managing Setbacks in Work and Life* (New York: Macmillan, 1998), pp. 3–4.

Chapter 3: Why We Are in Secondary Education

1. Olin, *Autobiography of St. Ignatius Loyola*, p. 83 n. 3.
2. George Will, "Micro-Solutions to Macro-Problems," *Baltimore Sun*, 3 January 1997.

Chapter 5: The Enduring Evidence of a Jesuit Education

1. Stephen R. Covey, *The Seven Habits of Highly Effective People: Restoring the Character Ethic* (New York: Simon and Schuster, 1989).
2. Robert Bolt, *A Man for All Seasons: A Play in Two Acts* (New York: Random House, 1960), p. xii.
3. Ibid., pp. xiii–xiv.
4. Robert K. Greenleaf, *Servant Leadership: A Journey into the Nature of Legitimate Power and Greatness* (New York: Paulist Press, 1977), pp. 75–76.

Chapter 6: Discernment: A Spirituality of Choice

1. Edward M. Marshall, *Transforming the Way We Work: The Power of the Collaborative Workplace* (New York: American Management Association, 1995), p. v.
2. Ibid., p. 86.
3. See, for example, the Jerusalem Bible.
4. Juan Alfonso Polanco, *Sumario de las cosas . . . a la institución y progreso de la Compañia*, in *Fontes narrativi*, 1:154, quoted in Dalmases, *Ignatius of Loyola*, p. 32.
5. Ibid.
6. Dalmases, *Ignatius of Loyola*, p. 23.
7. Ibid.
8. *Autobiography*, no. 8, as rendered by Dalmases, *Ignatius of Loyola*, p. 44.
9. From an address delivered at Loyola College in Maryland and reprinted in *Loyola* magazine (winter 1995, p. 16). Father Blaszczak was responsible for introducing young Jesuits of the New York and Maryland Provinces to Ignatian spirituality in the 1990s.
10. The Upanishads are philosophical writings from ancient India. I found this particular saying on a printed card without a source citation.
11. Cf. John C. Futrell, SJ, *Making an Apostolic Community of Love* (St. Louis: Institute of Jesuit Sources, 1970).
12. Kenneth Keniston, *Young Radicals* (New York: Harcourt, Brace and World, 1968), p. 275.
13. Jonathan E. McBride, "Manager's Journal," *Wall Street Journal*, 9 December 1985.

Chapter 7: Living Generously in the Service of Others

1. G. K. Chesterton, "The Ballad of the White Horse," in *The Collected Poems of G. K. Chesterton* (New York: Dodd, Mead, 1938), p. 210.
2. G. K. Chesterton, *Heretics* (New York: John Lane, 1905), p. 119.

3. He may well have been thinking of these lines: "The men of the East may spell the stars, / And times and triumphs mark, / But the men signed of the Cross of Christ / Go gaily in the dark." Chesterton, "The Ballad of the White Horse," p. 216.

4. William J. Byron, SJ, *Finding Work without Losing Heart: Bouncing Back from Mid-Career Job Loss* (Holbrook, Mass.: Adams, 1995).

5. Bernard Lonergan, *Method in Theology* (New York: Herder and Herder, 1972), p. 301.

6. James F. Keenan, SJ, "Proposing Cardinal Virtues," *Theological Studies*, December 1995.

7. Tom Mahon, "The Spirit of Technology," *Timeline*, May/June 1996, p. 11.

Chapter 8: The Celibate: A Crowd of One

1. *Documents of the Thirty-Fourth General Congregation of the Society of Jesus*, decree 8, no. 21 (St. Louis: Institute of Jesuit Sources, 1995), p. 120.

2. These words, often seen on ordination memorial cards, are adapted from Karl Rahner, "Orders: Vessels of Clay," in *Meditations on the Sacraments* (New York: Seabury Press, 1977), pp. 61–62.

3. Harold Kushner, *When Bad Things Happen to Good People* (New York: Schocken Books, 1981), p. 5.

4. Ibid., p. 136.

5. Ibid., p. 141.

6. Ibid., p. 143.

7. Ibid., p. 147.

8. Whereas the "harder" virtues like justice and fortitude can get a bit "noisy" at times, the Pauline criteria are "quiet" virtues, but virtues nonetheless. They embody strength. They reinforce assertiveness when appropriate, and they support a quiet competitiveness. They are not to be mistaken for sentimentality or what I think of as "cotton candy" spirituality.

9. "For the Sick," in "Masses and Prayers for Various Needs and Occasions," part of *The Sacramentary* [the Roman Missal] (New York: Catholic Book Publishing, 1974), p. 916.

10. John Henry Newman, "Meditations on Christian Doctrine," "Hope in God-Creator," in *A Newman Treasury: Selections from the Prose*

Works of John Henry Cardinal Newman, ed. Charles Frederick Harrold (New Rochelle, N.Y.: Arlington House, 1943), pp. 356–57.
11. Quotations from the Constitutions are cited in the text with the abbreviation listed below. The number following the abbreviation refers to the section where the quotation can be found.
    Const: The Constitutions of the Society of Jesus and Their Complementary Norms: A Complete English Translation of the Official Latin Texts (St. Louis: Institute of Jesuit Sources, 1996).
12. Dorothy Day, *Loaves and Fishes* (Maryknoll, N.Y.: Orbis Books, 1997), p. 209. This book was originally published by Harper and Row in 1963.

Chapter 9: Individuarians

1. Mary Douglas and Steven Ney, *Missing Persons: A Critique of Personhood in the Social Sciences* (Berkeley and Los Angeles: University of California Press, 1998), p. 122.
2. Patricia Wittberg, SC, "Ties That No Longer Bind," *America*, 26 September 1998, p. 12.
3. The source of this quotation is the second paragraph of the text of a talk given by Father Arrupe on September 3, 1983, at the 33rd General Congregation. See *Acta Romana Societatis Jesu*, vol. 18, fascicle 4 (Rome: Curia of the Society of Jesus, 1984), p. 987. These words appear on the reverse side of a memorial card picturing Father Arrupe at prayer. Beneath these words is a prayer for Pedro Arrupe's canonization bearing the imprimatur of Cardinal Adam Maida of Detroit.

Chapter 10: Stewardship: The Jesuit Approach to the Use of Wealth, Power, and Talent

1. William J. Byron, SJ, *Toward Stewardship: An Interim Ethic of Poverty, Pollution, and Power* (New York: Paulist Press, 1975).
2. Review of *Cyril Connolly: A Life*, by Jeremy Lewis, *New York Times*, 18 October 1998.
3. Ibid.

4. In a homily delivered at Saint Peter's College in Jersey City, New Jersey, on the occasion of the college's centennial celebration in 1972, then superior general Pedro Arrupe, SJ, said, "If I may leave you with a personal parting word, it is that you stress three things: first, a belief, a *confidence* in the abiding importance of what you are doing; second, a shared and practical and deep appreciation of the unique educational heritage that is yours; and finally, what Jesuits four hundred years ago called *cura personalis*, the concern, care, attention, even love of the teacher for the student—in an atmosphere of deep personal trust." There is no way in the world that these qualities will continue to characterize our schools without the commitment of dedicated lay colleagues willing to steward the tradition.

Chapter 11: The Standard of Christ

1. *Formula of the Institute*, no. 1. See *Constitutions of the Society of Jesus*, p. 3.
2. Pedro de Leturia, S.I., *Estudios Ignacianos* (Rome: Institution Historicum, S.I., 1957), 2:15. In the original Spanish, the sentence reads, *"Era además el Rey viviente y activo que no ha terminado aún la empresa encomondada por su Padre de conquistar todo el mundo, y que para terminarla busca hoy como ayer cooperadores generosos y Amigos íntimos que a tal jornada envié."*
3. John Kenneth Galbraith, *The Affluent Society* (Boston: Houghton Mifflin, 1958), p. 88.

Chapter 12: The Harvest Is Ready

1. See, for instance, Dean Hoge, *Future of Catholic Leadership: Responses to the Priest Shortage* (Kansas City, Mo.: Sheed and Ward, 1987). For a recent roundup of research, see Bryan T. Froehle, ed., *CARA Compendium of Vocations Research* (Washington, D.C.: Center for Applied Research in the Apostolate, 1997).
2. The closest printed version of this expression that I have been able to find is "Academic professors are interested in thought, not in action. So we have on the one hand thought without action and on the other action without thought." Peter Maurin, "A Third Open Letter

to Father Lord, SJ," in *Catholic Radicalism* (New York: Catholic Worker Books, 1949), p. 44.

3. James J. Gill, "Despondence: Why We See It in Priests," *Medical Insight*, December 1969.

ABOUT THE AUTHOR

William J. Byron, SJ, is University Professor of Business and Society at St. Joseph's University in Philadelphia.

He previously served as president of St. Joseph's Preparatory School (2006–2008); research professor in the Sellinger School of Business at Loyola College in Maryland (2003–2006); interim president of Loyola University in New Orleans (2003–2004); pastor of Holy Trinity Catholic Church in Washington, DC (2000–2003); distinguished professor of the practice of ethics in the McDonough School of Business at Georgetown University (1993–2000); rector of the Georgetown Jesuit Community (1994–2000); president of the Catholic University of America (1982–1992); president of the University of Scranton (1975–1982); dean of arts and sciences at Loyola University in New Orleans (1973–1975); associate professor of social ethics at Woodstock College (1969–1973); and assistant professor of economics at Loyola College in Maryland (1967–1969). He holds a doctorate in economics from the University of Maryland, two theology degrees from Woodstock College, and a bachelor's in philosophy and master's in economics from Saint Louis University.

After military service in the army's 508th parachute infantry regiment (1945–46) he attended St. Joseph's College (now university) in Philadelphia and entered the Jesuit Order in 1950. He was ordained a Roman Catholic priest in 1961. He is the author of twelve books and editor of two.